You May Already Be a Winner

You May Already Be a Winner

and Other Marginal Considerations

Jan C. Snow

The Kent State University Press

Kent, Ohio, and London, England

Library of Congress Catalog Card Number 92-3869

ISBN 0-87338-467-9

Manufactured in the United States of America

Illustrations by Aaron Sutherland

Library of Congress Cataloging-in-Publication Data

Snow, Jan C.

You may already be a winner, and other marginal considerations / Jan C. Snow.

p.   cm.

Includes index.

ISBN 0-87338-467-9 (alk.) ∞

I. Title.

PN6162.S658   1992

814'.54—dc20   92-3869

British Library Cataloging-in-Publication data are available.

This book is dedicated with thanks to any number of people, including (but not limited to) Mom and Dad, Dr. Bob, James Patrick "yes, he's Irish" Murphy, my weird niece in Indiana, Marsha Leigh, Vivaldi, Roger, Nancy and Karen, Danny Boy's Pizza, The Nitty Gritty Dirt Band, and, of course, Santa Claus, all without whom this book still would have been possible, but less probable. (Well, strictly speaking, I guess this book wouldn't have been possible without Mom and Dad because if it weren't for them, I'd be somebody else, and if I were somebody else I would have written a completely different book. Or maybe just been a computer programmer.)

Contents

Contents

Introduction:
You May Already Be a Winner

I REALLY have enjoyed writing this book. It's been fun and I sincerely appreciate all the cards and letters I've received, although I could have done without the fruitcakes. Anyway, I thought I ought to let you know that this book may be my last. You see, in just a few days, I could be a millionaire.

Yes, it's true. I could be a millionaire. I got the letter just yesterday. "JAN C. SNOW," it says right on the envelope, "YOU COULD BE A MILLIONAIRE!" All I have to do is put the gold validation seal on my entry certificate and mail it before the deadline and I could be a millionaire this time next month, in which case I'll probably be too busy jetting to Monaco for lunch or having my cheekbones redesigned to even think about writing another book.

"JAN C. SNOW—CLEVELAND, OHIO—MILLION DOLLAR WINNER!" the certificate reads.

Actually, I don't live in Cleveland. I live in Lakewood, an inner-ring suburb on the south shore of Lake Erie one municipality to the west of Cleveland. I wonder if that matters? If it does, I'd be willing to move. After all, what's a few blocks one side or the other of West 117th when you're talking about a million dollars? I probably wouldn't be spending that much time at home anyway, what with the condo in Aspen, the hideaway on St. Thomas, and, of course, the trips to Monaco.

"CONGRATULATIONS, JAN C. SNOW," the letter begins. I think it's nice that the people who sent me this letter know my name. I wouldn't feel right about accepting such a generous gift from complete strangers.

"JAN C. SNOW, YOU'RE AT THE TOP OF THE WINNERS' LIST," it says in the second paragraph. They use my full name throughout the letter—seven times in all. Even the salutation reads, "DEAR JAN C. SNOW." I think that's nice. In a world where sales clerks call me "honey" and waiters with whom I haven't the slightest inclination to form a relationship tell me their first names, all this formality is quite refreshing.

Each of the twelve prize tickets has my name—"JAN C. SNOW"— printed on it, too, right above one of my personal prize numbers. No one else has any of these numbers, the letter tells me. I'm the only one.

This worries me just a little. If no one else has these numbers, what happens if my twelve prize tickets get lost? Or stolen? Some people would do a lot for a million dollars. Maybe I should rent a safety deposit box and put the twelve prize tickets in there. Or I could buy a fireproof home wall safe from Sears and have it installed behind one of my bookcases. (I probably should put it behind the one with the fiction in it, alphabetized by author. Who would suspect anything important behind a paperback copy of Erich Segal's *Man, Woman and Child?*)

On the other hand, it might just be best to hire a twenty-four-hour security service. I can probably afford it. If I paste the surprise early-bird bonus sticker on the lower left-hand corner of the certificate before I mail it, an additional $100,000 could be mine. Although I lack direct experience with such sums, even I know that a million dollars plus a $100,000-surprise-early-bird bonus adds up to a lot of money. (I wish I'd taken the Lakewood Recreation Department's evening course last fall in personal investments.)

"DON'T DELAY, JAN C. SNOW. MAIL YOUR ENTRY NOW!" the letter warns. I have to tell you, all this pressure is getting to me. These people have no idea what my various obligations are. Although their offer seems generous on the surface, they're creating a moral dilemma by urging me to shirk my responsibilities and pursue wealth willy-nilly.

What if we all left what we were doing in order to stick gold validation seals on prize certificates? What if everyone in the country stopped working in order to paste a surprise early-bird bonus sticker in the lower left-hand corner, just to win an additional $100,000?

Think of it. No new rock-music videos would be produced. Manufacture of battery-operated electric socks would grind to a halt. Shamu, the killer whale, would miss his four o'clock feeding. I ask you, is even a million dollars plus an additional $100,000-surprise-early-bird bonus worth such social upheaval?

"JAN C. SNOW, DON'T MAKE US GIVE 'THE SNOW MILLION' TO SOMEONE ELSE!" the letter warns me. I don't know what to do. It's quite possible that the someone else who would receive "the Snow million" if I fail to return my prize certificate before the deadline really needs the money much more than I do. True, I'm a writer. I'm not rich. But I have enough to be choosey about what I eat and to pay the mortgage on the house in Lakewood with some regularity.

On the other hand, that someone else could be Queen Elizabeth, the richest woman in the world. (What would she spend it on? More hats and gloves?) Or, perish the thought, Nancy Reagan. Or even Cher. She's already had her cheekbones redesigned. I think I could make better use of a million dollars plus an additional $100,000-surprise-early-bird bonus than any of those people.

Perhaps I *should* take the time to paste the gold validation seal on the certificate. I probably ought to put the surprise early-bird bonus sticker in the lower left-hand corner, too. In fact, I think I should do those things right now. And mail my entry TODAY.

(You'll know. Either you'll see another book in about a year, or you'll get a card from Monaco.)

Constructive Criticism

For Whom the Bell Rings

I F there's one thing we of the late twentieth century do not suffer from, it's a lack of personal expression.

Bumper stickers ("Don't blame me—I voted for the other guy") and vanity plates (MACHO1) tell us more than we want to know about our fellow motorists. I used to live in a community where, year after year, one family's vehicle sported the license plate "WESKI." Seeing it always made me want to call the Ohio Department of Motor Vehicles and order up a plate that read "IDONT," but only because "WHOCARES" had too many letters.

T-shirts spell out our associations and vocations ("Do it with a photographer and see what develops"), leisure pursuits ("Mid-America Masochists Marathon"), and philosophies ("Life is uncertain, so eat dessert first"). My favorite is "Neurotic and proud," with "If it's physical, it's therapy" (courtesy of the American PT Association) a close second.

Now it's phone numbers. Our local telephone company, ever eager to provide us with new services (for a small monthly charge, of course), is extending our communications options by making available to us something called the custom listing, a service already in place in more progressive areas. "Lots of fun, prestige, and quick and easy recall," says the flyer. "A custom listing is prefaced with 'Remember that as' and is located directly below your telephone number in the white pages directory."

An example is "Jones Glen M.—555-4536," followed by "Remember that as 555-GLEN." What this means is that for no set-up charge and a mere $2.50 in perpetuity you too may have a four-letter word as your phone number.

My phone number could be (it isn't, but it could be) 521-SNOW. If it were, my directory listing would read "Snow Jan C.—521-7669," followed by "Remember that as 521-SNOW." You could also remember that as 521-RMNX, which is probably something really rude in an obscure Balkan dialect, or even 521-PNMY, which might even be worse, but I don't see how either would help much if you were trying to remember to call me.

Of course, you can't have a real honest-to-goodness four-letter word like 4355 (Remember that as HELL) or 3266 (Remember that as DAMN) for your phone number. The micro-mini print at the bottom of the flyer clearly states, "Ohio Bell reserves the right to reject any custom listing when, in its sole judgment, such a listing is objectionable . . ."

I'm sure they'd never allow 7448 (you figure it out) or even 2727. And if your phone number is 3825, you better have it changed right away. It's possible that 4674 (Remember that as GOSH) or 3276 (Remember that as DARN) might be permitted, but I have no way of knowing. You'll have to take that up with 6262 (Remember that as MAMA, as in MAMA Bell).

This could be fun, but I'm afraid I'm going to need more than one phone number. I don't really want to give everyone in the local calling area an identical message. There are certain people I'd love to have remember my number as 521-CALL or 521-HERE, but just as many to whom I would like to be 521-BUSY or 521-GONE. Most days 521-FINE would be appropriate, but on others anything more than 521-SOSO would be overstating the case, and there are times when nothing but 521-HELP would do.

I'd like to be remembered as 521-NEAT or possibly 521-COOL. (I know that dates me, but so do most aspects of my person.) I know better than to go for 521-CHIC or even 521-CUTE. They'd get me for some sort of truth-in-advertising violation.

While we're dealing with accuracy, let it be said that there are more guys whose phone number should be 5375 (Remember that as JERK) than there are telephone exchanges in the state. Ditto for 6373 (Remember that as NERD). Obviously the phone company stands ready to protect us from obscenity in our white pages, but what safeguards are in place to prevent the assignation of phone number/words that might mislead? What's to keep someone from choosing to be remembered as STUD when anyone who's ever met him knows he should be remembered as SPUD?

We've barely touched on the possibilities. More than just a number, your phone listing could include your name (PAUL—ANNE—RUTH), vocation (SELL—COOK—BANK), hobby (READ—BOAT—HIKE), or even personal qualities (NICE—RICH—EASY). If I didn't elect 521-SNOW as my custom listing, I might want my phone number to translate as TYPE, TALK, or even BEME (as in I've gotta . . .) But I think the number I would have to choose to express my thoughts on custom listing is 3862 (Remember that as DUMB), only because 74559 (Remember that as SILLY) has too many letters.

The Green, Green Grass of Home

AS the fragrance of charcoal lighter is the summer's signature perfume, the season's keynote is the sound of the lawn mower. Each weekend, an army of mowers is deployed to subdue the turf. Battalions of edgers, clippers, and weed whackers provide back-up support, and the air is alive with the whir, hum, and buzz of millions of tiny blades of grass being mechanically decapitated.

Most of us don't consciously acquire a lawn. What we set out to acquire is a house (excuse me, a home), forgetting that along with the American dream comes the American nightmare of a troublesome expanse of worthless vegetation that will dominate our leisure hours during the summer months. In fact, obtaining a lawn is a lot like having a baby or installing an in-ground swimming pool. Once you've got it, you have to take care of it for the foreseeable forever, which is usually a good deal longer than it takes for the novelty to wear off.

Lawn maintenance is clearly one of the more curious aspects of human behavior. It's obvious that if we were to plow the crab grass under and plant potatoes in the front yard it would be a better use of the space, yet still the otherwise intelligent among us persist in mowing and clipping, watering and weeding.

This necessity to maintain areas of short grass around our homes has been explained by some as a vestigial need arising from our aboriginal past in the savannas of Africa. Supposedly it has something to do with being able to see our enemies coming. I take this to mean that subconsciously we're afraid that if we let our front lawns grow IRS agents could hide in the tall grass and sneak up on us while we are sitting in our living rooms drinking iced tea and watching "Monster Trucks" on ESPN.

Whatever the reason, we are given to squandering substantial amounts of time, energy, and even money, all for the sake of growing something we can't eat, can't sell, can't trade on the world market, and can't even rollerskate on.

Even more curious than the need to maintain short vegetation around our homes is our penchant for maintaining only certain kinds of short vegetation, diligently seeking out and destroying all others, regardless of their height. Some dive into the trenches and attack the weeds one-on-one with hand tools. Others farm out the dirty work and hire professional assassins armed with chemical weapons. (It would be an improvement if we could learn to recognize crab grass as inevitable and make wine from the dandelions. Acceptance is the key to better mental health.)

As for alternatives to cutting the grass, consider these alternatives to growing the grass, most of which have been developed over the years in Tucson, Arizona. Although, I'm sorry to say, there is still plenty of grass grown in Tucson, with an attendant squandering of water, really sensible desert dwellers cover their front yards with Astroturf—Astroturf or indoor-outdoor carpeting of a verdant hue. Green gravel is another favorite, often artistically interspersed with cacti. I suppose stones would work, too, but my vote goes to concrete.

Even if you don't live in Tucson, why not pave the front yard? Pave it, and paint it green if you like. It will never need mowing or clipping, watering or weeding. You won't have to dump poisons on it and it will always look tidy. You still won't be able to eat it or sell it, but at least you can rollerskate on it. And you'll still be able to see the IRS agents sneaking up on you.

Sumer Is Acumen In,
Loudly Sing Ah-choo

SUMMER is a time for sailing and swimming, a time for picnics and porch sitting (when you're not cutting the lawn), a time for the sound of the Beach Boys and the smell of charcoal lighter, a time for figuring out how in the world to stay warm.

Logic would dictate that keeping cool ought to be the main task related to personal comfort in the summer, but this is not the case. Even with global warming, the greatest challenge of the modern summer is keeping from freezing to death.

Summer in much of this country is what summer is supposed to be—hot. By eight in the morning on a good July day, the mercury can rise high enough to send the digital time and temperature sign in front of the bank into malfunction. And the season can have sauna-like properties. The humidity rises along with the temperature and you can take fifteen pounds in water weight off your thighs just by walking to the corner mailbox too fast.

But that's outside. Inside, where you must necessarily go to transact the majority of your everyday business, there is climate control. Inside, in retail and service establishments, in restaurants, financial institutions, entertainment facilities, and even libraries, we must deal with systematic atmospheric adjustment. We must endure "air conditioning."

"Air conditioning" is a technical term referring to the mechanical maintenance of the interior environment at a temperature only slightly higher than that recommended for cryogenic preservation of cadavers. Vast amounts of costly energy, most of it generated by nonrenewable fossil fuels, are squandered in order that we may have goose bumps and blue fingernails from June to September.

Even I understand why banks have to be kept so cold. That's so the money won't mold. And department stores are maintained at a uniform 58 degrees Fahrenheit so that customers won't suffer heat prostration while they're trying on the winter coats that are on clearance at this time of year. That makes sense to me.

But why are supermarkets so cold? All the food that might spoil if it got too warm is already under refrigeration, isn't it? The watermelons and cucumbers in the produce area are chilled, the mozzarella cheese and yogurt are in the dairy case, and the pizza bagels and fish sticks are safe in the freezer.

Why freeze the stuff on the shelves? Why freeze the canned tomatoes and Hostess Ho-Hos? Everybody knows Ho-Hos can't spoil no matter what you do to them. Is it that freezing extends the shelf life of canned tomatoes? If that's the case, let's just put them in the freezer with the pizza bagels and the fish sticks so we can warm up the store a little.

Maybe stores refrigerate their atmosphere thinking that we, like gelid motor oil, will be unable to move quickly. Supercooled, we will stay in the store longer and spend more money. Perhaps movie theaters are kept frigid with the idea that lower temperatures will prevent crowds from becoming unruly, a real hazard given the quality of most movies. But if that were the case, businesses wouldn't bother to heat their premises in the winter. There has to be another answer.

The real reason it's so cold inside everywhere during the summer is that the thermostats of such establishments are controlled by bosses and managers. And these bosses and managers are either businessmen, or businesswomen dressed like businessmen.

Take a good look at the average male manager in business attire. Even in July, he's wearing long trousers instead of shorts and a long-sleeved shirt topped by a long-sleeved jacket instead of a light cotton T-shirt. Even when the mercury rises high enough for the annual slow-news-day trick of frying an egg on the sidewalk, he's wearing heavy shoes and socks instead of sandals. And then he tops it all off with a tie that snugs his collar to his neck with the efficiency of weather stripping.

The women are no smarter than the men on this one. They may not wear neck ties but they lose their advantage by draping their dress-for-success suits and tailored jacket dresses with silky scarves of nonpermeable polyester. They replace the long trousers with potentially cooler skirts, and then throw it all away by stuffing their lower extremities into pantyhose. You'd think somebody smart enough to earn an MBA would have more sense.

It's the corporate dress code we're fighting here. To win the war against summer frostbite, we need to change the costume of commerce. Get the bosses, male or female, into cut-offs and huaraches, and we can throw away our midsummer mittens. Dress the managers in loose, single layers of natural fibers and we'll no longer need to pack parkas just to go shopping.

Of course, it's an innovation that will take time to implement. Even though the bosses and managers make more money than we do, we can't expect them to reform their warm-weather wardrobes until at least mid-February. That's when the summer clothes will go on sale.

How to Annoy People at Concerts

ANY ordinary boor can snore or talk out loud during a concert. But an intelligent person such as yourself, a person of subtlety and inventiveness, need not resort to such crude devices to annoy people at a concert. There are other ways, more insidious and creative ways, to annoy your fellow concert-goers.

Chew gum, and pop it if you know how. Simple, but effective. Bring a sizable supply of candy or cough drops to eat during the concert, each piece, of course, individually wrapped in cellophane.

Wear one of those wrist watches that beeps on the hour, or, better still, wear your pager, especially if you're expecting a call. If your watch has an alarm you can set, so much the better. Check out a recording of the concerto from the library the week before the concert. With careful planning, you can time it so that the watch goes off just as the soloist is poised to begin the cadenza.

Hum along with the soloist, or whistle the second violin part lightly through your teeth. Tap your foot to the beat or, if you can manage it, tap just slightly off the beat. It's difficult, especially if you're musical, but worth the extra effort.

One of the easiest methods of annoying people at concerts is to bring along a small child, one obviously too young to endure the evening's program. With absolutely no special training, almost any youngster of average intelligence can be counted on to kick the back of the seat in front of him incessantly and make funny sucking noises with his tongue during the quiet parts.

If you'd prefer not to spring for the extra ticket, try implementing this full-concert plan for creating really effective annoyance on a budget.

Arrive at the concert hall in plenty of time for the performance, but don't sit down. Instead, mill around at the back of the hall. And don't be tempted to take your seat when the concertmaster enters. Wait until the conductor reaches the stage. Then, just as the maestro steps onto the podium, sprint down the aisle to your row and squeeze past the knees of those patrons who are already seated. If the aisle of the auditorium is not carpeted, good running shoes with nonskid soles are advisable.

Once in your seat, take your time about getting settled. Make a big production out of removing your coat and wiggle around a lot. (If the luck of the draw has rewarded you with a squeaky seat, be sure to note the row and number so you can request it the next time you order tickets.) Stretch your activity so as to make it last as far into the first movement as possible and then, with the exception of the coat removal, recapitulate your entire performance after the intermission.

If you're not athletically inclined, you may wish to try this more scholarly approach. During a soft passage, be overcome with the need to see who the bass player on the second-to-last desk is. Ruffle through your program until you locate the roster page. Mime your intense satisfaction at locating the information, repeatedly jabbing the page with your finger. Then, slap your program shut and drop it into your lap from a height of at least three feet. If the piece has more than one quiet section, you could look up the composer's life dates, the birthplace of the soloist or the latest additions to the patrons' list following the same procedure.

Annoying those around you at an outdoor venue such as Tanglewood, Blossom, or Wolf Trap isn't as difficult as it might seem. While effective, you needn't rent a light plane to circle overhead during the performance. It's expensive and, besides, it's been done.

If you're seated in the pavilion (or, at Tanglewood, the shed), many of the techniques that work well for indoor concerts can be adapted to this setting. Removing cellophane wrappers from candy during the adagio works almost as well here as it does indoors and, if you're attending the concert with a group, you can always

pass something—binoculars or a can of bug spray, for instance—
all the way down the row, and back again. Try to do it at least once
during each movement.

Out on the lawn other tactics are needed. Whistling Frisbees
are outmoded and crying babies are unreliable. (They tend to
sleep during the soft movements when they would be most useful.) Instead, bring along a portable radio. Tune it to the baseball
game and set the volume just high enough so that those around
you can hear the play-by-play, but can't make out what the an-
nouncer is saying. An even more sophisticated technique is to
tune in a symphony broadcast, choosing something being played
in a different key, preferably just a half-step lower or higher than
what's being played on the stage.

Although an electronic watch can't be heard well on the lawn,
you can pop corks or pull tabs on beverage containers. Also, try to
open and close your picnic cooler every few minutes, being sure
each time that the top is securely latched.

Of course, none of this applies to rock concerts. A Phantom
bomber circling overhead wouldn't annoy the audience at a rock
concert; in fact, they'd probably think it was part of the show. The
only possible way to annoy your fellow patrons at a rock concert
would be to insist that they sit down and be quiet and allow you to
listen to the music. But then, why would you want to do that?

Creeping Cutetrification

URBAN blight was big news in the seventies. Urban renewal, which we soon realized really meant urban removal, followed. Now our urban environment is suffering yet another kind of insidious deterioration. The neighborhood crisis of today is creeping cutetrification.

Cutetrification, like most urban problems, doesn't happen overnight. There are warning signs.

One of the first clues that cutetrification is about to become a serious problem is the bestowing of a name on the neighborhood. Instead of just those two blocks of stores on Broadway between Front Street and Washington Boulevard, suddenly you've got "Towne Centre," with an obligatory "e" on the end of each word. It's also obligatory that the commercial area be delineated by wooden signs proclaiming the new name in some sort of pseudo-Edwardian script.

One day there's nothing on the sidewalk but parking meters and a concrete planter full of wilted geraniums and cigarette butts. The next thing you know the merchants' association has painted the trash cans mauve and put curlicued wrought-iron benches out in front of all the stores. New street lights that look like Disney World copies of nineteenth-century gas lamps are installed. The whole neighborhood takes on the air of a theme park called "Boutique Land." (Excuse me—"Boutique Lande.")

Soon the corner deli that was really a deli—emergency groceries and racing forms in the back, artery-clogging, nitrate-laden cold cuts up front—is no more. It's transformed into a so-called deli where they put cinnamon in the coffee and serve tarragon-flavored chicken salad with artichokes instead of good, greasy corned beef, the kind of place dentists' wives dressed in tennis togs go for lunch.

After that, it happens fast. The bar where you could always duck in for a cold one and meditate on the neon beer signs turns into a stained-glass pub that takes reservations. The movie theater calls itself a cinema and sells subscriptions instead of popcorn. Before long the barbershop is gone, and the shoe repair guy retires and moves back to Hungary.

The hardware store closes and is replaced by a children's specialty shoppe called "Grandma Bait." The dry cleaner's disappears, and its place is taken by a store that sells nothing but decorative accessories in the shape of mallard ducks. The corner gas station hangs ferns in the cashier's window and changes its name to "The Fuelery."

Within less than a year, there are stores in your neighborhood that sell miniature vegetables, fresh-ground custom-blended coffee and 300 varieties of imported cheeses, but there's nowhere you can stop to pick up a box of Cheerios and a half-gallon of milk. You can walk down the block and blow your credit card limit on incredibly expensive clothing labeled "wearable art," but you can't buy a light bulb or get your boots resoled. There's a store that has hand-dipped, scented candles and darling little packets of potpourri, but nobody will sell you a can of Raid. You have to drive to the mall just to pick up three wing nuts and a ball of chalk line.

When it reaches this point, the battle with cutetrification is essentially lost. You might consider recruiting overweight volunteers to dress in pink and mint-green polyester pantsuits and hang around the shopping area to try and downscale things a little, but it's a long shot. Your only other course of action is to apply for a federal block grant and get funding to restructure your neighborhood by subsidizing an auto parts store, a mom-and-pop grocery, or, as a last resort, a 24-hour coin-operated laundry.

Bathtubs (Yes, Bathtubs!)

IN spite of its almost overwhelming abundance, ours is not a perfect society. Pantyhose run, dentistry is uncomfortable, airline food is a contradiction in terms, and bathtubs are incomprehensively primitive.

The configuration of the modern bathtub defies explanation and bears little relation to its function. The average tub is too short and too shallow, and unless you are a pigmy with substantial training in gymnastics, there is no way to soak all of your body parts simultaneously.

No matter how full you fill the tub, if your legs are underwater, your chest is out. Submerge your shoulders, and your knees breach the surface like twin whalelets. (It's not a pretty sight.) Lower those knees and your sternum reappears, high and dry. Slip your upper thorax back into the bath and up pop the legs again. There's just no way to win.

Such depth as there is, is at the end of the tub embellished by faucets, leaving you with the bulk of your bulk at the shallower of two too-shallow alternatives. It would make much more sense to put the drain and the faucets at opposite ends of the tub. At least the tub would be easier to clean.

But these are tubs built, apparently, for the convenience of plumbers, not bathers, better suited for occasional repair than daily use. As for the motives of those who design bathtubs, we can only speculate on what sort of childhood trauma might be responsible for such entrenched misanthropy, and look for a prime-time special on the problem during the next television ratings sweeps week.

No standard tub really can be described as comfortable, but some are a good deal less comfortable than others. The problem is, you seldom know what kind of a tub you have until it's too late to do much about it. This is because most of us purchase our bathtubs with houses (excuse me, I mean homes) attached to them. And while we count the bedrooms, scrutinize the foundation, pace off the kitchen, and peer into every one of the closets, few house hunters ever try on the bathtub. (The idea presents a pleasing picture, though, doesn't it?)

My most recently acquired bathtub, while attached to an otherwise fairly hospitable dwelling, is not only too short and too shallow but has a conformation which, like that of the wooden pews in certain Protestant churches, is guaranteed to prevent relaxation.

At the top is a ridge that digs into the unwary flesh of the back. Below this ridge, the surface of the tub curves away from the bather, a design suitable only for those with Quasimodo's peculiar posture problems. If you slide down and balance the base of your cranium on the edge, it gets the ridge out of your back but leaves you with no visible means of support for everything strung between your cervical vertabrae and your sacroiliac. Plus, as I've pointed out, your knees get cold.

Many people, due to their personal hygiene predilections, are completely untouched by these difficulties. That's because they take showers. All of us, it seems, can be sorted in a kind of binary fashion. We are women, or we are men; we are Republicans, or we are Democrats. And, in our most private moments, we are showerers, or we are bathers.

I am a bather. As far as I'm concerned, a shower is to a bath as the drive-through window is to a candle-lit table for two overlooking the lake: necessary at times, even desirable in certain circumstances, but hardly the same experience. In the Great Laundry of Life, I am not about to limit myself to the rinse cycle.

I like my home. It has a fireplace. It's on a quiet street, close to the park, and within walking distance of all essential services: bank, library, post office, and Taco Bell. It just has a terrible bathtub.

Had I tried on my bathtub when house hunting (still an interesting thought), I probably would not have been deterred from moving here. It's just that then I would have known what I was going to be getting into. Literally.

The Official List

FUNCTIONING at its utmost, the free press in a democracy serves up education, enlightenment, and a heap of thought-provocation. For example, I recently read in my morning paper that a bill has been introduced in Michigan that would adopt an official state soil.

Since this tidbit appeared in a brief editorial piece on official state songs, some readers may have dismissed it as an interesting typo. However, given the extensive list of official this-and-thats cluttering up the action in our fifty state capitols, we ought not to be too quick with that assumption.

Virtually every state has a state tree, the pine tree being the odds-on favorite. The plain old generic pine tree is the official tree of Arkansas and North Carolina. Exactly what ceremonial duties these official evergreens fulfill is unclear, but Minnesota so designates the red pine and Montana's official conifer is the ponderosa pine. Idaho and Maine each name the white pine tree as their state tree, but Maine takes the whole thing to a bit of an extreme. Not only is the white pine the state tree, the white pinecone and tassel is the state flower, and the state's nickname is "the pine tree state."

Nearly every state in the union has an official state flower and an official state bird. My almanac doesn't list any state flower for North Dakota, but it's not exactly an area noted for lush, colorful vegetation. That needn't deter the North Dakotans, though. Ohio's state flower is the decidedly non-native scarlet carnation.

Our state bird, the very native and similarly colored cardinal, is shared by Illinois, Indiana, North Carolina, and Virginia. The mockingbird is just as popular, representing Arkansas, Florida, Mississippi, Tennessee, and Texas. New Mexico has the only state bird to star in its own television show, the roadrunner. A cuckoo that runs on the ground, its Latin name is *Geococcyx californianus*, which explains the cuckoo part of it. California's state bird, by the way, is the California valley quail.

Pennsylvania has designated the Great Dane as its state dog, and Virginia's is the American fox hound. Oklahoma's official state reptile is the mountain boomer lizard, and a handful of Southeastern coastal states actually have official state shells. (You think I'm making this up, don't you?)

Idaho's state horse is the Appaloosa. Massachusetts also has a state horse, that being the Morgan, and Tennessee's is (what else?) the Tennessee walking horse. In New Jersey, where from the looks of things they're not very particular about much of anything, the state animal is just the horse. Any kind of horse.

Salmon and trout are favorites as state fish. Ohio doesn't have a state fish yet, but when we get one, odds are it will be the walleye. Moving on down the evolutionary scale, our state insect is the ladybug, revered for its habit of munching up garden pests. Connecticut's is the praying mantis, another renowned devourer of insect undesirables.

Both Illinois's and Pennsylvania's state insects, the monarch butterfly and firefly, respectively, are appealing creatures, but the honeybee is more honored than any other member of that vast six-legged class. Arkansas, Wisconsin, Nebraska, New Jersey, Vermont, and South Dakota all name the industrious little buzzer as their state insect.

South Dakota has an official one of almost everything you can think of including a state grass (Western wheat grass, since you asked), and Nebraska has a state fossil. So does Ohio. Nebraska's is the mammouth and ours is the trilobite, an extinct marine arthropod.

In Massachusetts, the state beverage is cranberry juice, and here at home, it's tomato juice. Either mixes well with vodka. Completing the category of official comestibles (along with the aforementioned official fish, both of which are tasty) is New Mexico, which has, believe it or not, two state vegetables. They are the chile and the frijol.

Maine's state mineral is tourmaline, which I had to look up. According to my dictionary, tourmaline (TOOR-meh-lin) is a complex crystalline silicate containing aluminum, boron, and other elements. Ohio's state stone is flint, and the state rock of Missouri is mozarkite, which I also had to look up but can't tell you anything about because it's not in my dictionary.

As for Michigan's official state soil, will it be loam, heavy clay, or sand, I wonder? Will it represent Michigan's soil as it is or Michigan's soil as those who care about such things wish it were? Will it be acidic or alkaline? Most nurseries and farmers are probably supporting a pH of six or seven, but the azalea growers are sure to lobby for something a little lower.

The curious aspect of all this is that in each case the state lawmakers have passed some sort of official legislation designating these various flora, fauna, and other flotsam as the official whatevers. I appreciate the amusement value of all this, but collectively it has to represent a great deal of time and probably a lot of money as well. Don't these people have anything better to do?

I mean, a state dog? It makes you wonder, doesn't it?

Music for the Masses

AS we've discussed, every state from Maine to Hawaii has an official state flower, state bird, state tree, etc. Some have gone so far as to name state dogs, state rocks, and, in the case of New Mexico, even state vegetables.

Collectively we have a national bird, a national anthem, and, as of a few years ago, a national flower, the rose. There's also the national guard, the national debt, the national pastime, First National, and Grand National, but we have no national musical instrument.

Some might suggest the piano, the musical instrument most likely to be found in the average American home. (Yes, I know there are probably more electric guitars in the land than pianos, but we're discussing *musical* instruments.) My nominee, however, is not the piano but the kazoo.

The kazoo is perhaps the only truly democratic instrument. Absolutely anyone can play it, a statement that you know cannot be applied to the piano if you've ever lived next door to a kid who was stalled in John Thompson's Red Book for two years.

With a kazoo there are no lessons to take. There's no music to read, no fingering chart to learn, and no embouchure to develop. A kazoo is ridiculously inexpensive to buy and purely simple to maintain. There are no reeds to make, no valves to oil and no bow to rosin. A kazoo never needs tuning and you can carry it in your shirt pocket. (Try that with a piano.)

The kazoo is not exactly big business, which may make it difficult to rally support to bring about official legislation on its behalf. Near as I can tell, in the whole country there's only one genuine metal kazoo factory (in Eden, New York, near Buffalo, since you asked). There are lots of plastic kazoos around, mostly cheap imported numbers, but we want the instrument that is going to embody our nation's musical identity to be a top-quality, American-made product, don't we?

Although the kazoo lobby is small, there is some ready-made grass-roots support for the kazoo right here in my northern Ohio backyard. Reasonably reliable sources report that the Chagrin Valley All-People Kazoo Band and the Olmsted Falls Marching Kazoo Band have been known to add their distinctive timbres to various local parades. And in Rochester, New York, where the winters are long and hard and there's not a lot to do anyway, an ensemble of kazooists called the Kazoophony has introduced the unassuming little instrument to higher musical society.

The kazoo could transform our society. Get every kid in the country to play a kazoo and, yes, you'll have to listen to the kazoos, but you won't have to listen to the kids. After all, it's hard to smart-mouth somebody with a kazoo in your face.

Adults should all carry kazoos not only for their entertainment value but in the interests of better mental health. Playing the kazoo would provide motorists stuck in rush-hour gridlock with some pleasant, nonhostile diversion. Regular kazoo breaks in the workplace could reduce stress and create valuable camaraderie among the office staff, and with fewer calories than donuts.

Kazoos could prove effective in the broader arena, too. Just think how the ceremonial presentation of a genuine American kazoo from Eden, New York, near Buffalo, to the President of the Russian Republic would set the tone at the next economic conference. He might play "If My Friends Could See Me Now." Then again, he might choose "Brother, Can You Spare a Dime?" In Europe, the Germans could adopt "Get Together" as their new anthem. Those in the Baltics might play "My Way" while the Hungarians toodled "Over the River and Through the Woods."

The Supreme Court Kazoo Octet Plus One (they already have matching outfits) might loosen up before the next abortion case ruling with a few choruses of "Baby Face." And an opening kazoo-for-all at each session of Congress would create a great deal more team spirit than whatever it is they're doing there now. (They'd probably play "Try to See It My Way," if they could ever agree on a starting pitch.)

Help, Self and Otherwise

CREDIT counselors and psychotherapists tell us millions of Americans shop obsessively for reasons that include boredom, anxiety, and anger. (Others shop obsessively for a plain tan raincoat, but that's a different problem.) Now there's a self-help group to aid shopping junkies, no matter what the reason for their compulsion. It's called Spender Menders. (You think I'm making this up, don't you?)

No human difficulty, it seems, need be endured alone. From Weight Watchers and SmokeEnders to Gamblers Anonymous and that granddaddy of support groups, Alcoholics Anonymous, good help is available to assist us in coping with our various addictions and behavioral aberrations. My favorite thought along these lines, though, is Anonymous Anonymous. ("Hi. My name might be Carol, and I'm an amnesiac. Or maybe my name is Barbara. Or Nancy Reagan . . .")

How about a group called Transistor Desisters? This one reaches out to adolescents who are learning to live without being plugged into rock music 24 hours a day. The process can be slow and painful, but recovery is possible. Members of this group follow a program of gradual withdrawal that begins with voluntary surrender of all heavy metal tapes, followed a week later by disconnection of the MTV.

Parents at any stage of the game need all the help they can get. Coach Quit offers hope for those who have served as T-ball organizers or pee-wee soccer league officials for two or more seasons in a row. A similar program is available for perennial room mothers (repeat offenders only) and those who can't stop volunteering to chair the Girl Scout cookie sale.

Young mothers who compulsively discuss their children's toilet training in public can join Toidy Talkers Anonymous. Using only their first names, which is all they can remember anyway, they learn that they are not alone as they share their experiences and gain needed social skills to reenter the adult world.

People who are unable to replace the cap on the toothpaste or the shampoo can begin to live better lives through Top Stop. Crease Cease is the answer for those who obsessively iron the plackets and collars of permanent press shirts. (It's not their fault; most grew up with mothers who ironed underwear.) Cigar smokers, being severely brain damaged from oxygen deprivation, are beyond help, self or otherwise, but motivated pipe smokers who sincerely wish to give up their untidy habit can find support in Tamper Stampers.

Many companies offer incentives to employees who lose weight or give up smoking. Add to that enlightened employers who offer Stop Chewing workshops for their gum-addicted workers. These efforts counter not only decreased productivity due to the intelligence-sapping potential of incessant, slack-jawed mastication, but also address difficult issues of lowered customer expectations and damage to the corporate image.

Alarmed by the spiraling cost of dental insurance and work time lost for bridge replacements, some companies even offer financial incentives. Workers who successfully complete the quit-chewing program and refrain from gum abuse for at least six weeks receive special bonuses. Monthly Chiclet Check-ins provide on-going support.

Aversion therapy workshops have proven beneficial to people who habitually punctuate their sentences with "you know?" Subjects are sequestered in small groups and provided with beer to drink and videotaped sporting events to discuss. When one says "you know," the therapist (or, if it's a good golf day, one of the therapist's assistants) administers a megavolt jolt to the offender through tiny electrodes inserted beneath the fingernails.

The same technique, with modifications, can redeem sufferers of other conversational tics, including people who finish your sentences for you and those who use the expression "passed away." Programs are now being developed for people who habitually tell everyone to have a nice day. The recidivism rate is high and, unfortunately, as of this writing, efforts to help saleswomen in the better dress department who call you "Honey" have been without success. But research is continuing.

Have a Day

I KNOW this is not a new issue. It's been discussed many times before, and stronger voices than mine have been heard on the matter. Nevertheless, I wish to say that I'm tired of being told to have a nice day.

It's really presumptuous. I mean, the person issuing this blandest of orders hasn't the faintest idea what kind of a day I would like to have. For all he or she knows, I may have a perfectly fabulous day ahead of me, a day of no deadlines, lunch at a good restaurant with a better friend, perhaps followed by a long, leisurely visit to the art museum. Labeling such a day as merely "nice" does it a tremendous disservice.

Then again, the day facing me may include a morning of root canal work followed by an income tax audit in the afternoon and dinner at my teetotaling, 92-year-old second cousin's house, the one who thinks all vegetables should be boiled for at least thirty minutes and that beef is done when it turns grey. "Nice" is asking too much of a day like that. A more appropriate send-off would be "Have a survivable day."

"Have a nice day" and its variant, "Have a good one," have become a sort of national conversational tic on a level (low—very low) with like, you know, the frequent insertion of "you know" into like every sentence and the prefacing of all clauses with, you know, the word "like." It's conversational pap, the verbal equivalent of that insipid little yellow smile face.

The kneejerk quality of "Have a nice day" isn't the nub of my annoyance, though. I agree with Miss Manners that the world runs more smoothly with the aid of predictable pleasantries. I sneeze, you say "Gesundheit." You say "Thank you," I say "You're welcome." Having part of the script already written saves us from the pressure of continuous ad-libbing.

Nor am I particularly bothered by the obvious lack of sincerity. I say "Hello. How are you?" and, thank goodness, you don't tell me. You say "Fine, thanks," no matter how you really are. I know that the chain-smoking kid who sullenly accepts my cash at the gas station doesn't really care whether or not I have a nice day. Furthermore, he knows that I know that he doesn't care what kind of day I have, but he tells me to have a nice day anyway. It's uttered on autopilot, without conscious thought. It's all just a matter of form.

No, what bothers me most about being told to have a nice day is the use of the imperative. "Have a nice day" is a command. You (subject implied) have a nice day. Whether you want to or not. No other option is discussed. If I am going to insist on dictating the quality of your life to you day by day, wouldn't you rather I told you to have an interesting day? Or, if you're really up, an intriguing day? How about "Have an exciting day," or even "Have a fascinating day"?

The worst thing about "Have a nice day" is that it lacks creativity. It reveals a deficiency of imagination and an impoverished vocabulary. Face it—it's boring. We need a little variation.

"Have a productive day" would be a good weekday-morning wish for most people. On Saturdays we could wish one another "Have a relaxing day," or maybe "Have a leisurely day." Now and then, I'd be willing to go for "Have an extraordinary day," but a lot of folks might be more comfortable with "Have a usual day" or "Have a satisfying day." I like that one.

"Have a routine day" might be welcomed by airline pilots and emergency room nurses. Someone who is feeling really stressed out might even prefer to be told "Have a dull day." Junior high school teachers and mothers of preschool children will appreciate "Have a quiet day."

Even if you decide, after adequate reflection, that you *would* like to have a "nice" day, I think it's important that we make it optional. "Have a super day." "Have a great day." Even a black-and-white generic "Have a day." There are lots of possibilities, but I don't really want the responsibility of deciding what kind of day you should have. I'm a Unitarian. Far be it from me to impose my values on you and tell you what kind of a day to have.

Still, I hope it's what you want it to be. Maybe we could agree on "Have a day of the quality of your choice." (That is, if that's what you'd like to have.)

Hearth and Home

Moving Right Along

A FEW years ago my personal environment was suddenly disrupted and rearranged as if snatched up and shaken by some giant cosmic hand.

I couldn't find my mixer. The control for the pink electric blanket vaporized. One very small but absolutely essential wing nut was AWOL from the desk lamp, and the sponge mop dematerialized. It was an extraordinary experience.

The beige dress and blue linen jacket that constitute one of my best downtown outfits were unaffected, but the blue-and-brown challis scarf I like to wear with them moved to another plane of existence. My skinny grey slacks and fashionably shoulder-padded purple shirt hung neatly in my closet, but I couldn't wear them because all I could find were tan shoes.

Sunspots? A dybbuk in the house? An acquisitive gremlin, perhaps, or maybe a pack rat with a flair for interior decorating whose blue and brown challis-lined nest was now furnished with a wing nut, an electric blanket control, and a pair of grey shoes?

No, the explanation was much simpler than that. You see, I had just moved.

Of course, most of my mail was late. The file with the insurance policies in it apparently had fallen into a black hole, and after the move the hallway clock ran slow. I adjusted and readjusted the tiny screw on the back of the clock and even changed the batteries. I couldn't seem to get it right no matter what I did, but it didn't concern me. After all, I'd just moved.

Maybe I should have been worried that I wasn't sure what time it was. (Does anybody *really* know what time it is?) Maybe it should have bothered me that I couldn't use the desk lamp or that I had to buy a new sponge mop, but it didn't. In fact, I didn't even mind wearing my beige dress and blue jacket without my special blue-and-brown challis scarf because I discovered in this experience the all-time, all-purpose, good-for-anything excuse. "I'm sorry," you say. "I just moved."

If you forgot about it or messed it up, all you have to say is "I just moved," and you're off the hook. If it's lost, if it's late, if you can't find it or didn't do it, say "Oh, I'm sorry. I just moved," and all will be forgiven.

No matter what the problem, as soon as people learn you've recently relocated, they ease their demands and begin to murmur sympathetically. If you've just moved, you can skip your nephew's piano recital and your sister will still speak to you. You can postpone paying your dentist by telling the office you never received a bill and would they mind sending a copy to your new address, please, thank you very much.

Work it right and someone may volunteer to drive your turn with the soccer car pool. (It's worth a try . . .) You can take two bags of plain potato chips to the P.T.A. potluck as long as everyone knows you've just moved. You might even get away with being late to work for a whole week, especially if your phone hasn't been installed yet.

When you've just moved, you can forget to go to a meeting you didn't want to attend anyway, and no one will fault you. And if you do go to the meeting, you can gracefully avoid accepting any office or committee assignment by saying "I'm sorry, but I just moved."

While no one would think of asking you to host a meeting when you've just moved, that's the time to volunteer because you needn't worry about having the house neat and clean, let alone impeccably appointed. Everyone will be suitably impressed if only you've cleared a bit of floor space and managed to find enough chairs.

Having all of your material possessions stowed in mostly unmarked cardboard cartons makes carrying out the business of everyday living somewhat difficult. People know this, and they're willing to cut you a little slack. But not forever.

Estimates vary as to how long those around you will tolerate "I just moved" as an excuse. A few will lose patience after only two or three weeks, but chances are they're the kind of people who alphabetized their stuffed animals when they were toddlers. It's safe to ignore them, unless, of course, you're married to one of them in which case I can't help you and you should have known better anyway.

A more realistic time frame calls for you to begin phasing out "I just moved" at about eight weeks. After six months it's advisable to stop using it as an excuse for all but the most exceptional circumstances, although you can still call on it for major disasters involving seasonal equipment such as snow blowers and plastic wading pools.

Some say that if you really want to push it you can get away with "I just moved" for up to a full year. At that time, however, your friends will be so sick of it they will do you physical harm if you so much as mention a change-of-address card.

After a year, if you want to keep on using "I just moved" as an excuse, you'll have to move again.

It just might be worth it.

Cracking the Code

I 'LL concede to the current doomsayers that America's performance in math and science education is pitiful, but anyone who laments the decline of creative writing skills in this country obviously isn't in the market for a house.

I'm not either, but I was not too long ago and I can tell you that there's a tremendous pool of literary creativity to be had in the nation's real estate agents. Some of today's most imaginative prose can be found in the real estate ads.

A home (they never call them houses—it's always a home) described as a four-bedroom, two-bath colonial is really a two-story, three-bedroom, one-bath house with an attic, plus a shower in the basement. "Finished third" refers to an attic with a floor and one bare light bulb. "Room for expansion" is the same attic with a light bulb but no floor.

Beware of the words "cute" and "cozy." Either can mean you have to schedule your family to be home in shifts. "Compact" or "efficient traffic pattern" means you can only live there if you're single and lose some weight before the deal closes.

An "eat-in kitchen" has room for two stools in the corner. "Formal dining room" means there's a wall between the kitchen and the space that has room for two stools in the corner. "Full basement" usually refers to the size of the cellar but takes on added significance in areas prone to heavy spring rains.

"All modern" assures you there *are* bathroom fixtures. "Well-maintained," the bathroom fixtures work. "Newly updated," they painted before they left.

"Many possibilities" tells you there are about two dozen code violations on the house. "Potential unlimited" means you'll have to do at least $10,000 worth of repairs to the place before you can even consider moving in. "Needs lots of TLC" covers many less drastic situations but may also refer to either of the above conditions, depending on local tradition.

"Loaded with charm" usually means the house is too old to have any insulation. "Original charm" means the house is too old to have any insulation and there's only one electrical outlet per room.

"One of a kind" could mean almost anything. That's been said about my weird niece in Indiana, too, and believe me, it's not always intended as a compliment.

"Ample storage" lets you know most of the bedrooms have closets. "Newly decorated," they painted before they left. "Custom decor," they painted before they left and everything is chartreuse except the bathroom, which is salmon and black with gold accents.

"Street of fine homes" tells you no one's screen door is falling off. "Family area," there are enough preschoolers on the block to open a branch campus of "Romper Room." "Executive area" can signal that the homes are overpriced but may simply mean none of the neighbors have been arrested this week.

"Outdoor living," there's a front porch. "Mature plantings," you can't see the front porch for the bushes. "Landscaped yard," they put in a flat of petunias and cut the grass. "Wooded lot," there are two small evergreens and a Japanese maple that won't make it through the winter.

"Convenient location" means right next to the freeway. "Easy access to highways," the master bedroom faces an on-ramp. "Near all conveniences" may mean there's a burger joint with a 24-hour drive-through next door. Or it could mean the house (oops—I mean, the home) is on a major transit line and a city bus rumbles by the front door every hour, on the hour, day and night.

"Country living" tells you there are no sidewalks and you'll have to drive the kids everywhere. "City view," the living room overlooks a used car lot that's open from 9:00 to 9:00 every day, including Sundays.

"Good starter home" means no one would live there except somebody who can't afford to live anywhere else. "Immediate occupancy," they've been trying to unload this one for two years. "Reduced to sell quickly" means "immediate occupancy" didn't work.

As for "move-in condition," it means they painted before they left.

Toothpaste (Yes, Toothpaste!)

THIS piece is about toothpaste. It's pretty ordinary stuff, toothpaste. Everybody knows about toothpaste because everybody—well, almost everybody, and certainly anybody *we* would know—uses toothpaste on at least a daily basis.

Not too many years ago, if you were an apartment dweller you really knew about toothpaste. You knew that when you were ready to move, toothpaste was what you used to fill all the nail holes in the walls so you could get your security deposit refunded. (Typing correction fluid, you might be interested in knowing, is helpful for disguising other sorts of blemishes, especially on woodwork, but that's another topic.)

All you needed was a small tube of plain white toothpaste. You just dabbed a little on your finger and smeared it over the hole. The excess was wiped off with a clean finger, bringing the filling material level with the surface of the wall.

That's all there was to it. No sanding, no tools, no skill and no special equipment—just toothpaste and an index finger, stuff even the least handy among us could deal with. For cleanup, you rinsed off your finger.

Following application as described, the toothpaste dried hard as a rock and quickly assumed the off-white color of generic apartment walls. A corollary benefit was the light mint fragrance it left behind, adding an additional aura of cleanliness to the place, which you hoped would aid you in your efforts to get your security deposit refunded.

No doubt the toothpaste method of wall patching is just as workable today as it was in my student apartment-dwelling days. The problem, however, seems to be in finding a small tube of plain white toothpaste.

I did some research on this at the Discount Drug Mart in beautiful downtown Lakewood. (Anything to get out of the office . . .) Cluttering the shelves between the mouthwash and the dental floss I found dentifrice in dizzying variety, very little of which is plain white. The most prevalent sort seems to be aqua-colored gel. There's also blue gel, red gel, green gel and one described on the package as "winter-fresh" gel. I'd expect that to be a sort of a light, slushy grey, wouldn't you?

Of course, no matter what their color, all these trendy gels are unsuitable for mending nail holes in apartment walls. And toothpaste that is old-fashioned opaque tends to be an up-to-date off-blue rather than the classic off-white necessary to the job.

One especially interesting brand is an imaginative combination of gel and opaque paste arranged in green, white, and red stripes. It oozes out of the tube onto your brush looking like an Italian flag and promises to do everything for your mouth but improve your vocabulary.

Yet another intriguing formulation is a basic white paste alive with tiny green sparkles. This stuff looks more like a material for Christmas crafts projects than a dentifrice. It has real possibilities. You could outline seasonal designs on a sweatshirt with it or use it to coat rubber Mason jar rings for clever tree ornaments. It might even be fun to use on your walls, but it would never get your security deposit back for you.

Not only is plain, opaque white toothpaste hard to find, small tubes of any sort of toothpaste are scarce to nonexistent.

Besides the trendy new pumps, most of which are full of the aforementioned off-blue stuff, toothpaste is readily available only in super-size tubes and family-size tubes, both of which are on the large side. Large-size tubes are really only medium-size, and the truly small ones, when you can find them, are labeled either medium or personal size.

No matter what size tube it comes in, toothpaste is handy for a number of odd jobs besides patching nail holes. Although you can't use it on your apartment walls, even off-blue toothpaste will take many kinds of ink off your skin. It will also, I'm told, remove skid marks from some vinyl floors. (I don't see much point to that unless you're willing to address the issue of how those skid marks got there in the first place. I mean, what exactly is going on in your kitchen, anyway? Tractor pulls?)

You can use toothpaste, probably of any color or degree or opaqueness, to clean jewelry. It is reputed to do a fair job on old marble lamps and tables, too. It'll get the smell of onions out from under your fingernails. And if there's any left over, you can always use it to brush your teeth.

As for your security deposit, you're on your own.

A Penny Saved

THERE'S no question that making ends meet these days is almost as much of a challenge as finding a parking place at the mall. Real income has been falling since 1973, but even as the dollar declines, you can come out ahead if you consciously cultivate frugality.

By applying yourself, you can develop a mind-set that will make you ever-alert to the myriad money-saving opportunities which surround us. All it takes is a little creative thinking.

For example, if you're short on hangers, don't head over to K-Mart to buy some. Instead, round up a bunch of winter coats, wool skirts and three-piece suits, and send them to the dry cleaners. (Some will even pick up and deliver, saving you gas.) You'll get plenty of free hangers and—an additional bonus—lots of plastic bags.

Speaking of bags, buy enough groceries (everybody has to eat anyway, right?) and you can forget about throwing your money away on expensive Hefty sacks. Some supermarkets will even double-bag your groceries, giving you both a brown paper bag and a plastic bag. While this is sort of packaging overkill on their part, it's a definite plus for you, the thrifty shopper.

Shop smart when replenishing your wardrobe, too. A $450 designer suit on sale at a downtown department store for $300 saves you $150, a much better buy than a Shoppers Warehouse dress marked down to $60 from $75, which only saves you $15. (Whoever said money can't buy happiness just didn't know where to shop.)

When you're done shopping, instead of running up your utility bills by cooking an elaborate meal, go out for dinner. You'll also save electricity and hot water because you won't be using the dish-washer as much. To further control your water heating costs, join a nearby health club so you can shower there.

Save still more electricity by making a habit of taking in films at your neighborhood cinema rather than watching movies at home on television. And, don't forget, the popcorn you munch and crunch at the theater will have been popped with kilowatts paid for by someone else. (Enjoy!)

Get your reading material from your local public library and you'll end up with nothing to show for your trouble but overdue fines and maybe a cheap paper bookmark. On the other hand, if you buy those books from a book club, you can earn bonus points that will bring you a free volume for every dozen or so that you purchase.

If you're into tunes, keep your eyes open for music-by-mail clubs that operate in a similar fashion. You'll get free cassettes or CDs to add to your collection, and you won't have to deal with try-ing to get a parking space at the mall.

You can put that dollar bill in your own pocket instead of into the transit authority fare box by driving to work rather than tak-ing the bus or subway. And you really should consider buying a second car. A second car can be insured for as little as half of what you're paying to insure your first car, which will yield a savings of 25 percent per car. Not bad, eh?

When you shop for that car, stay away from the economy models. They may seem the better bargain at first glance, but re-member, buy a cheap car and you'll have to pay for necessities such as power steering, power brakes, FM radio, and air condition-ing. With a luxury car, these features are likely to be included in your sticker price at no extra cost to you.

When you travel, whether for business or pleasure, always stay in a hotel rather than with relatives or friends. Virtually every hotel offers you free writing paper and soap, plus shampoo and sometimes conditioner in those cute little plastic bottles. Some of the better hotels even give you a free shower cap, a shoeshine rag, complimentary coffee, and your very own copy of the *Wall Street Journal.* Believe me, all you'll ever get from your relatives or friends is a return visit.

Of course, the most obvious money-savers around are ordinary, everyday children. It's amazing, but true. Produce just one little rug rat and you can deduct a bundle from your taxable income right off the bat. Manufacture a sibling for that child and the IRS will let you deduct twice as much.

Think of it! Have three kids and . . . well, as you can see, the possibilities are endless.

Good Food

I JUST did my grocery shopping for the week. And among the foodstuffs that will sustain me for the next seven days is some tofu: cholesterol free, packed with high quality protein, loaded with calcium and iron, the epitome of healthful eating. Also utterly devoid of taste or character, but never mind. It's good for me.

So is the rest of the food I bought. There's water-packed tuna, salt-free seltzer, and a loaf of whole-wheat bread the size and density of a concrete block. I also picked up some brown rice, herbal tea, and skim milk. I've got low-sodium soy sauce, oil-free Italian dressing, and lite (their spelling, not mine) ricotta cheese.

I bought fresh fruit (no Alar-sprayed apples, please) and a cornucopia of vegetables including those cancer-preventing crucifers, cabbage and broccoli. I didn't buy any brussels sprouts, but a person has got to draw the line somewhere.

A few or so years ago, what we thought of as good nutritious food was a little different than it is now. Quantity-wise, more was always better. We never worried about too much fat or salt. Being a nutrition-conscious cook simply meant you didn't boil the vegetables too long. And we'd never heard of cholesterol.

Then, at least here in the midwest, a good breakfast was a big breakfast: eggs and bacon or sausage, hash browns, toast and jelly, and plenty of whole milk. (Adults substituted several cups of fully caffeinated coffee, with cream.)

Lunch was a grilled cheese sandwich (Velveeta or American slices on Wonder Bread) and a bowl of you-know-whose tomato soup, topped off with a mess of buttery Toll House cookies and more whole milk. And for dinner, meat: big, undisguised chunks of animal, with potatoes and gravy. Mom may have added some Jell-O, rolls and butter, and a few green peas, but it was the meat and potatoes that mattered.

Somehow we grew up. We hung around the drive-in scarfing up greasy burgers and fries, the adolescent's preferred version of meat and potatoes. We went away to college and studied sociology, psychology, and other -ologies fueled by mystery meat and a stunning array of white starches. We got through graduate school on spaghetti with meat sauce, French bread loaded with garlic butter, cheap Italian wine, and espresso that would hold a spoon upright. Then, the dietary dictates began.

Eat less animal fat, the American Heart Association commanded sternly. Just two eggs a week, and no more butter. Not so much red meat, said the American Cancer Society, and more fiber.

Eat less salt, said everybody, and only whole grains. Throw away your pale pasta, and no more white bread. Cut out caffeine and stop eating refined sugars. Limit your alcohol intake and just forget about dessert.

Read the labels for sodium content. Check the ingredients for tropical oils, arterial trouble from Paradise. Avoid hydrogenated fats, and look out for EDTA.

I listened to them all. In the morning (but not too early in the morning), I pour low-fat milk on my high-fiber cereal. I order plain broiled fish and fresh fruit for dessert, thank you, at lunch. Dinner is baked chicken (evil skin removed), steamed broccoli, and a big salad sprinkled with vinegar. For snacks, there's always plain popcorn.

Well, it may be good for me, but it isn't what I really want. I want steak. I want French toast and sausage (but not too early in the morning). I want entire bags of barbequed potato chips. I want blue cheese dressing the consistency of plaster of Paris.

I want good greasy fried pork chops, buttered corn, potatoes with sour cream, and for dessert, a slice of pecan pie with enough calories in it to sustain an Asian village for a week. Oh yeah—and a cup of coffee.

Most of all, I want bacon. I want lots and lots of bacon, bacon with nitrates, sugar, salt, gobs of saturated fat, and not one single redeeming quality, the existential inverse of tofu itself.

But I've read Jane Brody and I know better. I love sharp Cheddar cheese, but if I have a piece, I think I hear my arteries making little choking noises. Like the bacon, I know it isn't good for me, so I don't eat it.

I also think I hear some rebellious portion of my warped little mind subversively whispering the old joke about the gourmand who, when told by his doctor that avoiding the pleasures of the table would lengthen his life, replied, "What's the point?" This is not a new question, but a satisfactory answer has not been forthcoming.

In other words, will I really live longer eating tofu and steamed broccoli instead of fried pork chops and pecan pie? Or will it just *seem* longer?

The Most Important Meal
of the Day

I
T seems to me that while we're on the subject of good food, we probably ought to discuss breakfast. Nutritionists seem to be in general agreement that a good balanced breakfast is important for optimum performance during the day.

I'll go along with that. My idea of a perfectly balanced breakfast is a copy of the morning paper in one hand and, in the other hand, a mug of black tea of sufficient volume to equal the weight of the newspaper. After all, it's pretty hard to perform optimally or even minimally if you're not fully awake and fully informed.

But a newspaper and a mug of strong tea are not exactly what the nutrition Nazis have in mind for me. They want me to eat oatmeal with raisins in it for breakfast. They think I should eat corn flakes covered with sliced bananas, or maybe whole-wheat toast with low-fat cottage cheese spread on it. (These are not well people we're dealing with here.)

My hand-to-mouth coordination doesn't function well enough for me to want to risk eating much of anything too close to sunrise. And then, I really prefer cold pizza or leftover mu shoo to oatmeal with raisins in it. In fact, I prefer almost anything to oatmeal with raisins in it, especially in the morning when my system is vulnerable enough as it is, without asking it to face up to anything like a bowl of oatmeal. As for whole-wheat toast with low-fat cottage cheese spread on it, how could you even suggest such a thing?

It really isn't fair. People in other countries don't have to eat oatmeal with raisins in it for breakfast. In Japan, breakfast is usually rice and fish. In Holland they eat pea soup with big wedges of cheese for breakfast (I've never been to Holland—I read that in a book), which isn't as good as cold pizza or leftover mu shoo, but it's a lot better than oatmeal with raisins in it. Come to think of it, anything is better than oatmeal with raisins in it, except possibly whole-wheat toast with low-fat cottage cheese spread on it.

The British, of course, tend to be excessive about breakfast, wrapping their early-morning stiff upper lips around things like grilled kidneys and kippered herring, foods you might not want to eat for dinner, let alone breakfast. And in parts of Eastern Europe, breakfast is likely to be cabbage soup, beet soup, or even sauerkraut soup, but what can you expect from people for whom babushkas and orthopedic shoes are high fashion?

The French, surprisingly, are much more sensible, choosing to start the day with café au lait and a croissant, which is really just a roll and a cup of coffee anyway. That I could probably manage, although the language will never make any sense to me. All those letters that don't get pronounced . . .

Please don't misunderstand me. It isn't that I don't like breakfast. I love breakfast, especially when it doesn't include oatmeal with raisins in it or whole-wheat toast with low-fat cottage cheese spread on it. Breakfast is one of my favorite meals. Really, it is. In fact, it ranks in the top three. It's just that I prefer to eat breakfast when I can more properly appreciate it. Like somewhere around lunch time.

Like Mother Used to Make

TALK about food long enough and, sooner or later, you'll end up talking about your mother. It also works the other way around. Any in-depth consideration of Mom ultimately brings us back to food.

My mom is not a great cook. (Sorry, Mom, but reading Scott Peck and Leo Buscaglia has taught me that real love is totally honest.) Mom is not really even a very good cook. Adequate, yes. Competent, okay, but the woman doesn't even own a garlic press, so how serious can she be? She's just not into it. As far as Mom's concerned, cooking dirties up the kitchen, and we'll all just be hungry again in an hour anyway, so why fuss?

Nevertheless, my mother has cooked for lo, these many years, and she has developed her own culinary style. It's based primarily on keeping the mess to a minimum, a sort of *neatelle cuisine*. Mom chooses her cooking methods according to how tidy they are. Whenever possible, food is baked or boiled. My mother rarely broils and almost never fries. Her favorite recipes are those that say "cook covered." That way nothing splatters.

Mom also respects a certain orderliness on the plate. When I was growing up (or at least getting older every year), the majority of the meals served at our table were composed of clearly identifiable individual components. Meat loaf, peas, potatoes (baked, of course). Chicken (yes, baked), carrots, rice. Unencumbered by embellishments of any sort, Mom's meals had a certain purity of form—broccoli ne'er met hollandaise at our house—and, you always knew exactly what you were eating.

My mother's instinct to keep it simple most of the time was well taken. Her occasional forays into the fringes of culinary exotica tended to yield somewhat less-than-noteworthy results.

She made spaghetti from time to time, ladling over it a bland mixture of hamburger and tomato sauce that few sons of Sicily would recognize. Without the pasta but with kidney beans (and still underseasoned), hamburger and tomatoes became chili. In the realm of the vaguely Oriental, Mom's only dish was chop suey—cubed leftover pork roast in gravy plus mixed "Chinese" vegetables canned in Archbold, Ohio.

Being a thoroughly middle-American, middle-class, generic white bread family, we had no memorable ethnic specialties at our house. No homemade ravioli, no spanakopita, no knedlicky, kolbasi, or perogi. We ate two-syllable foods. Swiss steak. Green beans. Roast beef. Pork chops. Foods that ended in consonants. Solid, unambiguous stuff.

But Mom manages to create some memories, nonetheless. She turns out a decent Thanksgiving turkey, although the dressing could use a little more sage. Her secret is tenting the bird with foil so the oven won't need to be cleaned. My mother also does a tasty Easter ham. She's especially good with the spiral sliced ones that come from the ham store. (Nobody can put a ham on a platter like Mom!)

And she does exhibit an occasional flash of brilliance. Mom's pecan rolls—sweet, tender yeast dough armored in nuts mortared with carmelized brown sugar—are, as they say in some circles, to die for.

Not to impute selfishness to Mother, but I'm convinced she's as good at them as she is because sweet rolls are what she loves best. Mom's idea of a peak gustatory experience is a cup of tea and a sweet roll, consumed without ever looking up from whatever she is reading.

No romance novels or science fiction, please, but almost anything else goes. Thrillers, mysteries, biography, historical novels—you name it, my mother will read it. Were I to have her memorialized in marble, it is this characteristic pose I would request the sculptor duplicate: head lowered, eyes fixed on the page, left hand holding the book open, and right hand, gripping a sweet roll, poised midway between plate and mouth.

Thoughts of such a tribute prompt me to mention just a few of my mother's many sterling (alright—silver-plated but nevertheless gleaming) qualities. After all, cooking alone does not a mother make.

My mother does not chew gum. She sings on key, dresses acceptably, and usually behaves well in public. She does not clap between movements and wouldn't think of wearing white shoes until after Memorial Day.

Mom is a talented teacher, a dedicated soldier in the battle for literacy. She is a tireless volunteer. She's a good dancer and a decent typist. My mother is wonderful company and, as you might imagine, fairly well read, a lively conversationalist with a positively grade-A sense of humor.

She's also very tidy. Especially in the kitchen.

Dishing It Out

I T'S a part of almost every recipe. Sometimes at the top, more often at the bottom, it will say something like "Serves four."

Serves four? Serves four what?

Four prime-time women who are perpetually dieting? Four adolescent boys who are trying to bulk up to make the junior varsity football team? Four weary middle managers who spent all day in a motivational seminar at the Holiday Inn and in spite of the fact they don't even like molded fruit salad and beef tips Shanghai over rice ate too much for lunch because they were bored?

And what is this recipe for? That's every bit as important as how much of it there will be when you're done cooking it. If it's anything made with shrimp, it will just barely serve the number of people you are having to dinner, no matter how few. You can have three out of eight guests cancel at the last minute and still not have enough food if shrimp is the main ingredient.

Other foods provide an infinite number of servings, regardless of what the recipe says. Boiled cabbage is one of these, as is any sort of creamed leftover and stuff like tofu casserole.

No matter how little you make, one dinner never kills a tofu casserole. What's left takes on a life of its own and acts as an illustration of Zeno's paradox right there in the bottom of your refrigerator. People will eat some of it but they will never eat all of it, so no matter how much anyone eats, there's always some of it left. (This never happened in Zeno's refrigerator, of course, because he always finished everything, even the tofu casserole. But, that's a Stoic for you.)

And exactly when and where are you planning on serving this dish? Does this recipe serve four in the kitchen on Thursday evening when everybody has to leave in twelve minutes to get to a meeting, or does it serve four in the dining room on Sunday afternoon when it's raining outside and there's nothing good on television anyway?

Even more important is, what are you serving with this dish? This question is too complex to be dismissed easily.

"Serves four" may actually mean "serves four unless you are having soup first in which case you might be able to stretch it to six." Or, "serves four unless there's no bread in the house, in which case it will serve only three, unless one of you ate lunch after 2:30." Then, there's the worst case scenario: "serves four unless you didn't get home in time to make another vegetable and a decent salad and all you've got to go with this is half a pint of cole slaw from the deli so you'd better double the recipe."

Who decides what a serving is, anyway? Is there somebody at the National Bureau of Standards, Weights, and Measures Department, whose job it is to determine how much of various foods we are expected to eat at one sitting?

Designations like "makes four half-cup servings" aren't any more helpful than the basic "serves four." You still have to figure out who's going to be eating it when, where, and with what in order to determine if a half-cup is too much or too little to expect each of your eaters to put away.

Recipes for baked goods tend to approach the matter in a much more straightforward fashion. They simply give you the facts: "makes two loaves" or "makes one 12-inch cake." They don't try to interpret that in terms of its application to the various members in your household. It's up to you how you work it out and if you can eat the whole cake before the rest of them get home, it's all yours.

The molasses cookie recipe in my favorite big, all-purpose cookbook says "makes about 40 two-inch cookies." I never get that many because, except for the first few, I don't make them that small. Soon after I start, I tire of plopping neat little cookie-dough mounds in orderly rows on the baking sheet, and the cookies get larger and more irregular until the last sheet holds about four, each the size and shape of a baby elephant's ear.

Still, even though I never know exactly how many cookies I will get from the recipe, I can usually figure out how long they will last. I count how many of us are in town and divide by the amount of milk in the refrigerator. (Cookie consumption can be shown to be in direct correlation to the amount of milk available for dunking.)

That same cookbook gives the yield for caramel frosting as "enough to frost a two-layer cake." No mention is made as to the dimensions of this two-layer cake, nor is any consideration given to how thickly you're going to spread the frosting or whether or not you really like caramel frosting.

For fudge frosting, the authors are more specific: "yield, 2½ cups." I can tell you that's just enough to frost three small cupcakes. Unless, of course, you don't want to lick the bowl.

Double Exposure

NOBODY has any time any more. I don't understand it. Maybe the length of the day is being shortened by the expansion of the universe or something, or maybe it's just as long but goes faster, which might be the same thing. Whatever the reason, none of us seems to be able to keep up.

Business has not exactly rushed in to help us out. Sure, you can do minimal banking transactions (sorry, no home mortgages) at the supermarket or pick up bread and milk at the corner gas station, but those are hardly innovations on the level I'm seeking. I need real help, some way to cut the endless list of "things I gotta do today" down to size.

There is hope. A pair of entrepreneurs in (where else?) California has come up with "Clean and Lean," possibly the first combination coin laundry and fitness center anywhere. This is what we need, what I think of as a Certs-style operation. (It's two [clap], two [clap], two stops in one!)

The place has washers and dryers *and* aerobic workout machines and stationary bikes. Think of it! You could work yourself into a lather while the family linens launder. Firm your inner thighs and spin dry your socks at the same time. Flex your pecs and fluff your panties simultaneously. Now that's progress.

How about "Styles and Smiles," a combination beauty salon and dentist's office? It could be run by a husband-and-wife team. (I'll let you decide which does what.) Get your fingernails and your teeth polished in one stop. Have your root canal done while you're waiting for your spiral perm to develop. After all, you'd just be sitting there anyway . . .

"Katz and Dogs," a kosher delicatessen with a shoe department, could really increase your lunch-hour efficiency. Your hands could be busy with the corned beef sandwich while your feet, which normally would just be hanging out under the table, would be trying on the latest in pumps. The myriad possibilities for daily specials like half-off latkes and loafers or two-for-the-price-of-one bagels and brogans boggle the mind.

"Disks and Drums" is the perfect name for a brake service place with a computer store in the waiting area. Instead of wasting time thumbing through the October 1984 issue of *Corvette News* or shuffling through old copies of *The Elks Magazine*, you could shop for PC accessories for your home office. Familiarize yourself with the latest in small business spreadsheet programs or experiment with the color monitor while the 30 minutes they assured you it would take to replace your pads stretches into two hours. Or visit "The Mr. Goodwrench Executive Search Firm." They change your oil while you work on changing jobs. Have your resume and your transmission overhauled in the same afternoon.

While we're on waiting rooms, computer shopping terminals at the internist's would allow you to pursue constructive activity in the inevitable and inexplicably interminable interval between the stated time of your appointment and the moment the receptionist actually says, "The doctor will see you now."

Instead of fantasizing about committing imaginative but unspeakably hostile acts against the medical establishment, you could buy a complete spring wardrobe or solve the problem of a graduation gift for your weird niece in Indiana. Just think of the stress-reduction value! In fact, such patient-diversion facilities ought to be required by health insurance companies as contributory wellness factors, don't you think?

"Hash and Cash" might be a 24-hour diner with an automatic teller machine next to the register so you could get the money to pay for your meal at any time of the day or night without stepping outside. "Heel and Deal" would offer obedience training for your pet, opportunities in real estate investment for you. (For your convenience, all offices open evenings Monday through Friday, Saturday until 5 P.M.)

Learn to waltz while you work on your relationship at "Arthur Murray Couples Counselors." And "Yards and Yards"? A fabric store with a consulting landscape designer, of course.

Coupled with home delivery, such combination enterprises could further revolutionize our daily lives. Have your domestic environment spiffed up by "Mop and Mow," a housecleaning service that does lawns. Just be sure the franchisee has been carefully trained so workers don't put Weed and Feed on the old brown shag carpeting in the family room.

For analysis with anchovies, order in from "Little Sigmund's Pizza." Get a 16-inch pie with extra cheese and anxieties delivered by a psychiatrist who makes house calls. (Neuroses cured in 30 minutes or it's free.)

And then there's "The Novel Eye." (I really like this one.) I see it as a kind of bookmobile, a popular lending library with copies of all the latest, driven by a dispensing optician with a degree in library science. She parks in your driveway.

Instead of using a Snellen chart (that's the one that's in all the cartoons with the patient saying, "I can read it but I can't pronounce it"), the optician/librarian tests your eyes with this week's *New York Times* bestsellers list. ("Now cover your right eye and read the title next to Stephen King's name.") Then, while you check out a new supply of escapist literature, the optician makes your glasses.

And there you have it. Fiction fast, fiction right.

The One-Minute Minute

HAVE you got a minute? Sure, I know you're pressed for time, who isn't? But you must have a minute. Just one minute. Any minute will do, and one is all you need. You can do almost anything you want with it. (Before reading further, you might want to put on a recording of "The Minute Waltz.")

You've all heard of *The One Minute Manager*. We're not sure what she does with the rest of her work day—seven hours and 59 minutes by my calculations. She probably takes a long lunch. If she can do it, why can't we?

No doubt our one-minute manager got where she is today by reading *The One-Minute Salesperson*. I'll bet her assistant is a devotee of *The One Minute Business Letter* and *The One Minute Organizing Secret: Finding Electronic Files, Papers, Books and Almost Everything Fast*, which I presume means in one minute or less. I also presume whoever wrote that one has never seen my office.

Those of you with an intellectual bent might enjoy perusing *The One Minute Philosopher*. Before you get into that, though, you probably ought to read *One-Minute Methodology*, which I would assume provides the academic basis for all of this.

Still have some time? Sure, you do. You've only used six minutes so far, unless you administered "the one minute reprimand" after you studied *The One Minute Manager*, in which case you've used seven minutes. Either way, you have plenty of time left to enrich your leisure life with *The One Minute Game Guide* (no, I am not making these up), *One Minute Photo Lessons,* or *The One Minute Los Angeles Ticket Guide.*

(I don't understand that last one. Does that mean it will take you one minute to read the Los Angeles ticket guide? Or that this book will tell you how to get a ticket to Los Angeles in one minute? Maybe it tells you how to get a ticket that will allow you to stay in Los Angeles for one minute, which, as far as I'm concerned, is just about long enough. How about *The One Minute Hackensack Ticket Guide?* You don't want to stay there any longer than a minute, either. Or *The One Minute Columbus Ticket Guide.* The possibilities are endless.)

Now that you're so efficient, you can afford to invest a little time—very little time—in your personal life with *The One Minute Relationship,* which is about how long things seem to last these days, anyway. Or *The One Minute Lover.* On second thought, I believe I've already met him.

Certainly with all the time you're saving you have enough time to give your offspring the full 60 seconds they deserve. Check out *The One Minute Mother* or, if you are of the paternal persuasion, *The One Minute Father,* subtitled "A Father's True Story about the Quickest Way to Teach Your Children How to Like Themselves and Behave Themselves." That's all. It takes one minute just to read the title.

One-minute mothers and one-minute fathers no doubt administer discipline with a one-minute scolding and read their one-minute children to sleep with *One Minute Bedtime Stories.* When your 60-second darlings tire of those, there are *One Minute Favorite Fairy Tales* and *One Minute Animal Stories* to turn to. Members of Slow Talkers of America may want to use the condensed version so they won't run over the allotted time.

Now, just wait a minute—I've got a minute here somewhere— let me see if I can find it. Ah, here's one, but you can't have it. Sorry, that one is mine, my *One Minute for Myself: The Secret of Caring for Yourself and Others.* Wow, all in one minute! I wonder if that includes the dog?

But only one minute for myself? Just one? That's really a big disappointment. I had hoped to spend much more time than that just in the whirlpool.

Third-Class Bulk-Rate
Direct Marketing Material

I KNOW we touched on this earlier, but, like Alice's experiences in Wonderland, the contents of my mailbox get curiouser and curiouser.

Today's crop yielded some fairly normal stuff: information on poetry readings at a nearby university, a sale flyer from the Discount Drug Mart in beautiful downtown Lakewood, and a nice color brochure inviting me to test drive a new Toyota. (Do you suppose they'd let me drive it to Bloomington, Indiana? Now, that would be a test!)

The folks at the community center tell me they're producing a play for which they hope I will buy tickets. I've also been invited to purchase a subscription to a chamber music series, attend two crafts sales, sign up for evening activities at the high school (maybe I *should* take that class in personal investments), and hear a lecture by a famous historian at the Cleveland City Club. I'm probably not going to do any of those things, but it's nice to know everything that's going on that I can't attend.

Also tucked in my US Postal Service–approved wall-mounted delivery box was a chain letter urging me to "Kiss someone you love when you get this letter and make magic." The remaining instructions involve sending 20 copies of the letter to people I think need good luck. "After a few days," it concludes, "you will get a surprise. This is true even if you are not superstitious." I wonder if this also is true even if the person you kiss is not infectious?

A subscription solicitation from *Harper's* informs me, "You thrive on independent thinking. You're intrigued by events and ideas. And you read as much as you have time for." Actually I read more than I have time for, but how would they know? A similarly obsequious pitch comes from Master Chefs Institute and assures me I am "a person who enjoys the impeccable service and exquisite cuisine found only in the finest restaurants." Obviously I've been spotted walking out of the Lakewood Taco Bell.

Best of all is a catalog that contains among its many wares some great-looking rubber chickens, plastic tiki-god party lights, trick candy, four-inch Shriner dolls, glow-in-the-dark cockroaches, and, my favorite, the lobster hat. "Colorful foam lobster to wear on your head." (I think I'll ask for one of those for my birthday.)

None of this mail came from an individual who upon meeting me on the street would recognize and greet me. Although most of it had my name on it, none of it was sent by anyone who really knows who I am. All of it, every coupon, reply card, paper scrap, and torn envelope of it, is what's known as third-class, bulk-rate, direct-marketing material—i.e., junk mail.

Be it mundane or mondo weird, it isn't long before the mail begins to pile up. I know this happens at your house, too, so I have a few suggestions for putting your junk mail to good use.

Probably the easiest thing to do with your junk mail is to bundle it up in bales and throw it in the trunk of your car to provide traction on icy winter roads. Another cold weather tip: increase the R-value of your exterior walls by banking your junk mail around the edges of your rooms. If you're on as many lists as I am, you'll have enough to complete the entire job in about a week.

You could grind up some of your mail, combine it with water and self-rising flour, and use the mixture to create low-cost, non-representational sculpture. Or express your creativity by decorating your home with clever collages. A combination of National Rifle Association solicitations and Sears lingerie ads would be chic for the wall of the master bedroom. For the kitchen, try an artful array of grocery special fold-outs intermixed with carcinogen warnings from *The Vegetarian Times*.

If you get a lot of magazine subscription offers, you could stack the reply cards according to size and bind each stack tightly to form a kind of brick. When you have enough, build yourself a nice backyard gazebo.

To share the fun with those outside your household, take a few select pieces of junk mail to church with you. During the sermon, busy yourself by placing the mail so the hymnal will fall open to certain pages. For example, put the coupon for Listerine at No. 79, "Breathe on Me Breath of God." Slot the 25-cents-off Dr. Scholl's air pillow insoles at No. 132, "Standing on the Promises," or the advertisement for the Water Pik at No. 322, "Come Thou, Font of Every Blessing." You get the idea.

If you're not religious, attend the library of your choice and apply the same technique to the reference room. Put the Citizens' Alert toxic waste information in the Los Angeles phone book. Slip one of those postcards about lost children into the *Benet's Reader's Encyclopedia* at the entry on Sir James Barrie (think about it . . . it will come to you).

Those should be enough to get you started. Any mail you have left over could be soaked in water until pulpy, sprinkled with sugar, and set in a warm place. I'm not sure, but I think it will ferment.

Wonders of the Universe

Pockets

POCKETS are more than workaday luggage for our material minutiae. Even when conceived as design elements, they are not just embellishments or convenient places to hide our hands. Pockets are free zones in which the otherwise immutable laws of the universe do not operate as elsewhere.

Put a penny in your pocket and overnight it will become six. Put a quarter in your pocket and it will turn into two Canadian nickels and a piece of used Juicy Fruit gum. Put a crisp, new five-dollar bill in your pocket in the morning and by afternoon it will be replaced by an old one-dollar bill, rumpled and dirty, the upper left corner torn away.

Dark and warm, pockets serve as estuaries for minor matter such as shirt buttons and bobby pins. Rubber bands that remain sterile in desk-top organizers reproduce readily in pockets, and the paper clip supply of the nation completely replenishes itself every two weeks inside our pockets.

Pockets are defined not by their outsides, but by the spaces they surround. Within these spaces are small but significant areas of potent magnetic force. These unexplained energy fields can cause tops to float away from their pens and candy wrappers to unswaddle their sticky charges.

Also contained within pockets are processing plants for the manufacture of lint. All of the lint in the universe is created by pockets and clothes dryers. In pockets, lint is synthesized from

Kleenex combined with material extracted from the pockets' own linings and seemingly thin air, in much the same way that green plants synthesize organic compounds from carbon dioxide, water, and sunlight.

The closets of a house (excuse me, I mean home) are analogous to the pockets of a garment and provide breeding grounds for wire hangers and teenagers' tennis shoes. Instead of lint, closets synthesize dust and a certain amount of unclassifiable cosmic stuff, the origins of which are unknown.

Many pockets have hidden chambers, invisible to the human eye, where they stash "while-you-were-out" slips and business cards. These are released only after the pocket-bearing garment has been run through the wash at least twice. If particularly crucial information has been written on a phone message slip or the back of a business card, even in indelible ink, it will be dissolved by enzymes secreted by the pocket.

Pockets have the ability to transfer your personal items among themselves so that the car keys you left in the pocket of your blue blazer show up the next day in the pocket of your grey slacks. Not altogether serious, pockets sometimes indulge their sense of humor by doing things like moving an important tax-deductible receipt from the sport jacket you're wearing today to your pink and green Hawaiian shirt, the one you bought at the pool shop when you were staying at the time-share condo in Myrtle Beach three years ago and haven't worn since.

Many people have been confused by the appearance in their pockets of a rental brochure from a bicycle shop in Elkins, West Virginia, or a lunch receipt from the A&W Root Beer stand in Williston, North Dakota. They feel unnerved by the discovery of a cocktail napkin from The Flat Iron Cafe in Cleveland with "Angela— 984-7332" scribbled on it.

The explanation is really very simple. Within your pockets are tiny teletransport stations which receive objects beamed to them by pockets in places you've never visited. That's why even though you've never traveled out of state except to attend your weird niece's graduation in Bloomington, Indiana, pencils from Atlanta's Peachtree Plaza and matchbooks from Elwin's truck stop in Cairo,

Illinois, can show up in your pockets at any time. So can the take-out menu from Don Juan's Chinese Food, a kosher restaurant in Hendersonville, North Carolina, that went out of business six years ago. Just try not to let it worry you.

A Date with Destiny

My aspirin is going to expire. It says so right there on the side of the package: Expires 12/93. Sometime in December of 1993, presumably on the last day of the month, the life of my container of aspirin, a little slide plastic box of twelve tablets, will be over.

What will it do, I wonder? Will it call friends and loved ones to its bedside, wishing to have them near at the end? I can see it, all those longtime medicine cabinet mates huddled around, their little warning labels almost touching as they press closer to hear the poor aspirin container's dying words. What a way to celebrate New Year's Eve.

My lip balm is due to expire in August of this year. Maybe it will explode, marking its departure from the world with a loud noise, or perhaps it will just quietly disintegrate. Maybe it won't change at all. It'll just sit there in the tube looking exactly the same as it did before it expired. But if I use it by mistake after it expires, maybe it will poison me, or permanently glue my lips together. These are things to worry about.

My antacid is set to expire the same month as my aspirin. My mouthwash is slated to go seven months before that. According to the label, my antiseptic spray expired last month. I can tell you it went without a whimper. I didn't even know it wasn't feeling well.

I have one tube of sunscreen that was terminated in April of 1985, but my other tube of sunscreen has no expiration date on it. The stuff in these containers looks the same. It feels the same and it smells the same, but one is expired and the other isn't. What does this mean?

My cough drops carry no printed limit on their vitality. The house-brand generic nasal decongestant and antihistamine I buy doesn't have an expiration date either. I suppose that means it's good indefinitely, or the manufacturer realizes that with the number of viruses reeling around in the air this medication will be consumed long before it has a chance to age, let alone expire.

I know I come with an expiration date; I just don't know what it is. Obviously destined to outlast me are my deodorant, toothpaste, and hand soap. They don't have any expiration dates at all. My insect repellent, hair spray, and nail polish remover are certified as equally eternal.

My vitamin pills have no expiration date either. I find that disturbing. Years from now, I'm going to get a listing in the obits, but my One-a-Day multiples plus iron will still be going strong. Somehow that doesn't seem fair.

The Training of Cats

 MANY people believe that it is impossible to train a cat. This simply is not true. Cats can be trained just as easily as dogs, and quite a bit more easily than children. The secret is in using methods that are appropriate to the feline temperament, which in no way resembles that of either a dog or a child.

I had a cat once. Actually I had two cats once, but one of them didn't stick around very long.

Their names were Sam and Janet Evening. We were formally introduced by an enterprising eight-year-old who turned his wagon into a mobile marketing unit in order to divest himself of a sudden over-supply of kittens. Capitalizing on the innate cuteness of baby cats, he convinced me to pay him one dollar for the pair, delivery included.

Shortly after the beginning of our relationship, Janet left. Perhaps I did something to offend her. Anyway, I was never quite sure whether she decided to relocate in a better neighborhood or was eaten by the German shepherd across the street, but our paths did not cross again.

Sam, however, was with me for nearly a year and a half. Actually, to say that Sam was with me overstates the case. It also invites a misunderstanding of the nature of cat. More accurately, Sam and I coexisted in the same space for a time. That is, he suffered my proximity for 18 months in exchange for regularly extorted payments of premium cat chow.

During the time Sam and I were together, I developed numerous insights into the training of cats. I learned, for example, that it is not necessary to raise your voice when training a cat. Volume, you will find, has even less effect on a cat than it has on your children.

Neither does cat training require any investment in little pet yummies to be used as rewards. Unlike dogs and children, cats clearly are above bribery.

Like many endeavors in this life, success in cat training is mostly a matter of timing. For instance, if you command your cat to come when he is heading in the opposite direction, you are doomed to failure. Instead, wait until the cat is walking directly toward you; then call him.

If you would like your cat to stay, wait until he is sound asleep. Then, softly, so as not to disturb him, give him the command to stay. This technique is nearly foolproof. Likewise, practice giving your cat the command to go out only after he has scratched on the door. It's really very simple once you get the hang of it.

Give your cat the command to eat just as you set down his food bowl and he most surely will obey you. Once the two of you have mastered that, give him the command to come and the command to eat simultaneously. Unless you're trying to feed him really cheap cat food you should be successful.

I taught Sam to leave the room by giving the command every time I turned on the vacuum cleaner. Consistency, of course, will yield the best results.

Some cats can be taught to sing, but I don't recommend it unless you're trying to get out of your lease. Likewise, I don't advise teaching cats to dance. They always want to lead.

Fruitcake

THE theory has been advanced by some fairly responsible persons that there is, in truth, only one fruitcake in the universe: one lone fruitcake that is cycled endlessly from house to house, family to family; one fruitcake given and received, wrapped and unwrapped, year after year after year.

This is not true. If it were, world population being what it is, an individual would receive fruitcake for Christmas less than once in a lifetime. Unfortunately, it happens more frequently than that.

Most people who give fruitcake buy it from otherwise charitable organizations or from gift catalogs of gourmet foodstuffs, glossy little brochures filled with pictures of cheese-spread assortments, imported biscuits (cookies to us), and smoked turkey that goes for about the same price per pound as platinum.

This is misleading. After all, cheese spreads, imported cookie-biscuits, and ruinously expensive smoked turkey, while not your basic diet, are edible foodstuffs. Fruitcake is not a foodstuff. It's more like petrified stuff, once-upon-a-time organic matter now rendered inedible and indestructible by time and natural forces. That fruitcake is a food is a myth, much like the purported existence of rutabagas or the state of Indiana.

It is possible that fruitcake is botanical in nature, that it is the honest product of some well-meaning but misguided member of the plant kingdom. It may occur as tubers or even rhizomes. Many such things are not edible.

Or maybe fruitcake is alluvium deposited by prehistoric rivers, or the result of ancient lava flows from the Big Rock Candy Mountain. But it isn't food.

I'm inclined to believe that fruitcake is intergalactic, originating far beyond our planet and brought to earth eons ago by stray meteorites that crashed through our atmosphere to the ground, creating shallow craters speckled with candied citron and plasticized pineapple.

Perhaps it arrived with extraterrestrials who visited our world in ancient times, leaving no trace of their visit except the mysterious lines that form giant hieroglyphs on the Nazca plains of the Andes, and fruitcake. (Carbon dating of fruitcake indicates that most of it hails from the Paleozoic era, some time after the Devonian period but prior to the Cambrian, when much of the world's cheese was formed.)

What with all the fruitcake recipes in *The Joy of Cooking* and elsewhere, we are given to feel that fruitcake is baked, produced, or somehow assembled by human beings in kitchens. This is not true either.

Fruitcake more closely resembles a conglomerate—a rock made of loosely cemented heterogeneous material—than anything else. Given its geological characteristics, it seems likely that fruitcake is mined rather than baked. Veins of the stuff apparently were discovered in this country in the 1800s. During the great fruitcake rush that followed, vast quantities of it were extracted from the earth, mostly by elves of the sort whose descendants now bake cookies (not biscuits) inside of trees.

All of that fruitcake is still in circulation. Should you be seized with the urge to give a fruitcake to one of your friends (or, more likely, one of your enemies), consider secreting something in the bottom of it: a fishing sinker, a small ball bearing, or a modest Cracker Jack prize, perhaps. That way you can tell if the fruitcake you receive next year is the one you gave this year.

Should you receive a fruitcake, it is recommended that you store the cake wrapped in a brandy or wine-soaked cloth. Liberally reannoint the cloth with additional brandy every now and then. When it comes time to enjoy your fruitcake, wring the cloth over a small glass, send the fruitcake to Indiana, and just drink the booze.

A Natural History of Socks

AT first glance, socks seem to be relatively simple and straight-forward organisms. Each has a toe and a heel, a top and a bottom, an inside and an outside. No appendages, no complicated internal organs, just a simple tube closed at one end, yet their behavior is astonishingly complex.

Although socks vary widely in color, pattern, and size, they are almost all the same shape. Among the more important species within the genus are the wool argyle, the cotton athletic sock, and the synthetic dress sock, which includes a race of executive over-the-calf socks.

Most socks are native to the temperate zone, although some breeds, such as the ragg wools and the thermal insulated types, are indigenous to colder regions. Domesticated for tens of thousands of years, socks have been spread by humanity and catalogs to virtually all corners of the earth.

Many laypersons assume that socks are related to shoes, boots, slippers, and other footwear. In truth, they are more closely related to mittens. Clothing taxonomists also include knit sweaters as members of the same genus, an important characteristic of which is the ability to unravel in a single strand. A defining field mark is knit-one-purl-one ribbing.

The cuff, even when vestigial, as it is in ladies' low-cut tennis socks, is always present in true socks. Those tennis socks with little pastel pompoms above the heel are not members of another family but merely unfortunate mutations, as are socks with individualized toes. Knee socks, with or without cables, represent a localized adaptation to specific climatic conditions.

While not particularly intelligent, socks are extremely agile and have a well-developed sense of play. They can turn themselves inside out in the wash, crawl under beds, and leap out of the hamper onto the bathroom floor. In the dryer they particularly enjoy hiding inside pillow cases or hitching rides on nylon undergarments.

Some sock movements are migratory. On a seasonal basis, each succeeding generation of socks makes its way from the clothes basket to the floor behind the laundry tub. Whether the young socks learn the way from older socks or navigate purely by instinct is the subject of ongoing research.

Little is understood of the feeding habits of socks, although they are believed to be one of several median links in a food chain that begins with simple lint and ends with the Salvation Army collection box. In North America the sock's predators include vacuum cleaners and house cats.

Socks may be distinguished from other footwear in that they do not mate for life. And unlike pairs of pants, which almost never split up, socks seldom remain paired for more than a brief time.

In fact, one out of every three pair of socks is separated within five months. In California, it's one of every two pair. Socks have reached sexual maturity when they develop holes. Only those with holes reproduce in the wild, and these sexually-reproduced offspring have holes just like their parents.

Those without holes are created by asexual reproduction under carefully controlled conditions in sock factories. These socks are then temporarily paired and released into the domestic environment, to begin again the mysterious and wonderful cycle of life.

But Do They Do Windows?

GO stand next to your houseplants, the ones on the wooden stand next to the dining room windows. (Go on.) Now put your ear down next to the spider plant. Get in nice and close. Just lean over a little and listen closely. (Go ahead, do it!) Do you hear a kind of soft, whooshing sound? (Try harder.) Now do you hear it? That's your house plants filtering toxic gases from the air.

It's true. House plants can help you tidy up the place. Common, ordinary, everyday, potted greenery, it has been found, can purify the air in our homes. Even those of us who live out most of our lives in slovenly bliss are seized now and again with the desire to exert control over our domestic environments, usually when we find out Mom is coming to visit. Now, along with Mr. Clean and Mary Ellen, we have a new ally in the battle against filth.

Formaldehyde gas, the most common indoor pollutant, is emitted by some modern building materials and, like almost everything, is suspected of causing cancer. Well, put some plants into the room and within six hours they'll reduce the level of gas by at least half. Spider plants were found to be the most efficient, removing more than 90 percent of the formaldehyde within one day. Banana plants, peace lilies, and peperomias (peperomiae?) also did a pretty good job. (You think I'm making this up, don't you?)

This discovery comes to us from the nifty folks at NASA. Microbes found in the potting soil are responsible for part of the air-cleaning effect. The plants' stomata—those are the little holes in their leaves that they breathe through—do the rest.

Of course, for significant air cleaning, you need to scatter at least fifteen medium-to-large spider plants around your house, which makes for a lot of greenery. Three times as many peace lilies and four times as many peperomias (peperomiae? I'm still not sure) are required to achieve the same pollution control as the lower number of spider plants, but if you decide to go that route, you won't need to worry about cleaning anything. Everything in your house (excuse me, I mean home) will be covered with plants.

If we can get spider plants to clean the air, why can't we train the wax begonia to do floors? Perhaps the coleus could learn to clean the oven, or at least scrub out the sink. Maybe the asparagus fern would defrost the refrigerator, and the chenille plant is a natural to make the beds.

The rat-tail cactus could be assigned to pest control duty. The grape ivy, with its climbing capabilities, might be just the thing for washing walls, and the pigmy palm could dust with ease in small spaces and tight corners. As for the Chinese evergreen, provided with the proper equipment it might do an okay job on the living room carpet, but chances are an hour later it would just need vacuuming again.

Perhaps the usefulness of indoor plants isn't limited to housework. Might the aurora borealis plant serve as a night light? How about assigning the aloe plant to answer the telephone? (Get it? "Aloe? Aloe?") And while I admit I don't know what a sedge is, it sounds like something that could really come in handy if the plumbing backs up.

Of course, this whole concept is not without problems. Once it becomes known that house plants can serve as domestic servants, will it be considered racist to grow African violets? (Is it anti-Semitic to hang a Wandering Jew?) Maybe we're just asking for trouble. You'll have to get a Green Card for your Mexican snowball. Some big-time bleeding-heart-liberal senator will introduce a bill making it illegal to take cuttings without paying workers' compensation, and the next thing you know the inch plants will unionize and refuse to propagate.

Still, it would all be worth it if we could develop a geranium that'll do windows.

Up in Smoke

ONCE again, archaeological advances have shed important new light on a previously misinterpreted primitive culture. While it had been thought that the entire spiritual life of the Suburbanites, as these people were known, revolved around the veneration of large metallic objects called "cars," we are now certain that they also practiced ritual burning.

In most areas where the Suburban culture flourished, only mature males were permitted to preside over the burning ceremonies. Females often acted as acolytes, participating in the preliminary preparation of the flesh to be burned and bearing it on great platters to the male presiding at the altar.

Before burning, the meat was slathered with an unguent of tomatoes, sugar, and spices symbolic of the blood of the slain victim. The pyre typically was constructed of cubes of charcoal lavishly anointed with a purified distillate. Small sticks were set ablaze by rubbing them vigorously across a rough surface and flung in the direction of the anointed coals, the action accompanied by vociferous exhortations to the gods to send flames.

The procedure was repeated a minimum of three times. (Numerology was extremely important to the Suburbanites, as evidenced by the presence around their settlements of myriad numerically encoded paper talismans called "lottery tickets.") Often several additional anointings, followed by the flinging of more small fire sticks, took place before the actual burning began.

As the pyre-lighting ritual progressed, ever-stronger incantations were employed. So powerful were these chants that if a member of the uninitiated—a child, for example—should unwittingly repeat the words aloud, he would endure strict censure by the mature female of his family group. Such censure often included banishment of the child to his private quarters within the dwelling or the application of cleansing material to his mouth to "wash out" the taboo words.

Among the ritual objects associated with the burnings were scepter-like tools ending in multiple sharp prongs and long-handled flat metal trowels brandished by the priest during the ceremonies. An enveloping vestment was wrapped about his midsection, symbolizing the containment of his great power. Some priests also wore hats of abnormal height as a sign of their standing above other mortals.

Some of these vestments were crudely adorned, such as one recently unearthed which bears the legend "Caution: Man Cooking." Such decorations are believed to have been purely ornamental in nature and of no ceremonial significance.

Throughout the ritual cooking the priest sipped a sanctified beverage made of water and fermented grain. The beverage was contained in shiny metal cylinders inscribed "Michelob Light." (An astonishing number of these cylinders have been found, but the meaning of the hieroglyphic is yet to be deciphered.) Mature males other than the officiating priest also partook of the grain beverage, standing in a semicircle around the altar and thus participating vicariously in the burning.

These burnings most often took place during the Suburbanites' holy time, the "weekend," which was an outgrowth of earlier Sabbath celebrations. Some especially devout Suburbanites practiced midweek burning as well, and members of a fanatic cult in an area known as "California" are believed by some experts to have held burnings daily.

The altars themselves were fashioned in a variety of shapes and sizes, including some used for private devotionals. These were called "hibachis" in at least one dialect. The majority of the altars were movable, but others appear to have been fixed within the areas of short grass that typically surrounded the Suburbanites' dwellings.

Although basically non-nomadic, the Suburbanites sometimes made short pilgrimages, carrying portable altars with them to sacred areas on the edges of their villages where no houses (excuse me, I mean homes) were built. These sacred places were located adjacent to bodies of water or in forests. The pilgrimage represented an homage to the elemental forces of nature which the Suburbanites believed exerted tremendous control over their lives.

A key element in the planning of a pilgrimage was the consulting of a magic viewing screen contained in every Suburbanite's dwelling. If the hallucination seen in the screen predicted that the elemental forces would be favorably disposed to a ritual burning, the pilgrimage was made. If, on the other hand, the hallucination advised that the forces were likely to indicate their displeasure by calling forth thunderstorms or high winds, the pilgrimage would be postponed until a more propitious "weekend."

Certain sacred areas were fitted with row upon row of altars where mass burnings attended by vast numbers of the faithful were held. These burnings were a part of the observance of the Suburbanites' three major festivals, celebrated at the beginning, middle, and end of the warm season.

Associated with the burnings was the belief that mortals could, by imitating the sun's fire, capture the warmth of summer and thus prevent its departure from the earth. Another component of the burning mythos was the idea of smoke as a heavenward vehicle for prayers.

Although no contact between the two cultures can be demonstrated, the Suburbanites may have shared with the Saharan Nemadi the belief that the soul of the dead beast resides in the bones. Instead of casting them aside for the children and dogs, the Suburbanites saved the bones. Bundled in protective plastic shrouds with other revered objects, the remains of the ritual burning were transported to gigantic middens, probably on a weekly basis, by a privileged class of men charged with their collection.

Broccoli and History

OVER the years, we've focused our national paranoia on an astonishing array of real and imagined enemies. We've worried about being invaded by Martians or attacked by killer bees. We've cowered before onslaughts of Asian flu and Australian mosquitoes, and, until recently, communism was dangled before us as the ultimate peril.

Yet all the while, one invader was making substantial inroads into our great country with little notice. Quietly and with great stealth, it infiltrated the heartland of our nation, meeting virtually no resistance along the way.

The real menace, my fellow Americans, is not red, but green. And its name is broccoli.

Broccoli is inescapable. Broccoli is unavoidable. Broccoli is everywhere. Unadorned, and too often underdone, it graces virtually every contemporary restaurant dinner plate as the inevitable "vegetable-of-the-day." Sometimes it is broccoli braised or broccoli stir-fried. Most often it is broccoli steamed. (We will not discuss broccoli boiled.) Restaurants with perhaps more pretention and less regard for the American Heart Association's latest recommendations cloak the ubiquitous green stalks with hollandaise sauce or cheese sauce, but underneath it's still broccoli.

Not limited to playing sideman to the entree, broccoli makes its appearance elsewhere on menus as broccoli quiche, broccoli frittata, broccoli sauce for pasta, and cream of broccoli soup. (Please tell me no one is pushing broccoli pizza.) As for crudités, order that and you'll just get a bunch of raw vegetables, with broccoli sure to be among them.

As you probably can tell by the vowel with which its name ends, broccoli, like Vivaldi and cheap red wine, is a gift from the Italians. Until the 1920s, says vegetable historian Bert Greene in *Greene on Greens*, no one in America had ever heard of broccoli except those who emigrated from the plant's warm and sunny homeland. The name probably is derived from *brocco*, Italian for twisted thread or shoot, or it may be a corruption of the Latin *bracchium*, which means arm. (*Bracchiolum*, by the way, means little arm. It's sort of beside the point, but isn't it cute?)

Either way, a little broccoli, we must admit, might be a good thing. Heavy on the vitamin A and reasonably rich in potassium, broccoli (*brassica oleracea italica*, botanically speaking) belongs to that family of vegetables which includes the humble cabbage and appears to reduce the risk of certain cancers.

Although they hadn't the benefit of such knowledge, Caesar and the other imperial Romans nevertheless are said to have enjoyed broccoli more than daily. In fact, Greene says they may have eaten it as often as twice or even three times during a meal, which brings us back to where we began.

Take heed, America. We concede that correlation does not prove causation. But as you meet broccoli at every turn, on every plate, and in every guise, meditate briefly, if you will, on the fall of Rome's once-mighty empire.

Junk Drawers

E VERY household has at least one.

Sometimes it lives in the generic family desk that fills the corner of the living room where nothing else fits. Or it may nest in that small chest of drawers in the front hallway at the bottom of the stairs.

But while it may survive nicely in those places, the preferred habitat of the junk drawer is in the kitchen. Given free range of a house (excuse me, I mean home), most junk drawers will choose to settle under a Formica counter, in close proximity to the silverware drawer, and not far from the toaster oven. There a junk drawer will not merely survive, but thrive.

The location of a junk drawer can't be determined arbitrarily. You may make a conscious effort to assign it to a particular place, but unless that's where your junk drawer really wants to be it won't stay there long. Bit by bit, rubberband by push pin by capless ballpoint pen, no matter where you take a notion to settle it, a junk drawer will move itself to that which it feels is its proper place.

By nature, a junk drawer is driven to seek out its own niche in the ecosystem of your home. Go ahead and move it elsewhere if you're really into power-tripping. You won't win. Sooner or later the junk drawer will end up right back where it wants to be and there isn't a thing you can do about it.

If you live in a colonial—which for this discussion means any dwelling where the bedrooms are upstairs and the rest of the house is downstairs—chances are your domestic environment will spawn two or more junk drawers, a minimum of one for each inhabitable floor of the dwelling.

Upstairs hallway or bathroom junk drawers are likely to harbor illegibly labeled plastic prescription vials containing two pills each, matchbook-size sewing kits with names of insurance agencies on them, and little bars of soap from the Orlando Holiday Inn, plus, of course, rubberbands, push pins, and ballpoint pens with no tops. This is also the place to look for the instruction manual and warranty card for the electric toothbrush you left at the time-share condo in Myrtle Beach three years ago.

Bedroom junk drawers tend to reflect the personality of the owner of the bureau in which the junk drawer is housed. Mine (since you asked) is currently home to an inoperable Mickey Mouse pocket watch, a couple of black plastic spiders that were intended to be part of a Halloween costume, a $10 gift certificate for a Cleveland department store that went out of business in 1984, some half-filled (half-empty if you're a pessimist) books of Green Stamps, and lots of coin wrappers, rubberbands, push pins, and pens with no tops.

It also holds an autoharp tuner. I don't have an autoharp, but if you do and you'd like me to tune it for you, give me a call.

A survey of my kitchen junk drawer reveals still more coin wrappers, a lot of plastic bread bags, equally as many wine bottle corks (mostly Gallo with a few Riverside Farms and one stamped "Bully Hill Vineyards—wine without guilt"), a crippled screwdriver, take-out menus from every cheap restaurant in Lakewood, and, inexplicably, a TV program schedule with ESPN's "Muscle Magazine" circled in red.

There are also several old shopping lists. My personal favorite reads "Q-Tips, lettuce, milk, caulking, and pickles," plus of course, rubberbands, push pins, and pens with no tops.

All of these things are where they are because junk drawers are scavengers that eat things no other drawer will have. Like catfish, junk drawers are bottom feeders, prowling the lower level of our hierarchy of possessions, scarfing up thumbtacks, incomplete decks of playing cards, misplaced Monopoly tokens, and half-eaten (half-uneaten if you're an optimist) packs of butterscotch Lifesavers.

Junk drawers feed on household flotsam—miniature golf

scorecards, singular garden gloves, and coupons (usually expired) for cinnamon-flavored instant oatmeal—the jetsam of daily life. They grow strong on simple fodder like paper clips and garbage bag twist-ties. And they have a minimum daily requirement for rubberbands, push pins, and pens with no tops.

The masking tape and string that you think are supposed to be in the junk drawer never are. The drawer's immune system recognizes these truly useful items as inappropriate transplants and rejects them.

What will remain in a junk drawer are things that are hard to classify, things that you don't really have any use for right now but that are too good to throw out, things like little paper salt and pepper packs from fast food joints and a nearly new purple crayon.

Some things gravitate to the junk drawer by virtue of a perceived potential: an odd-size glasses case, a pair of pink plaid shoelaces, and something that looks as if it might be an elephant condom but is really the nylon carrying sheath for a folding umbrella.

Junk drawer dwellers often are of uncertain pedigree: batteries whose power is suspect, keys that fit no known lock. Still other things end up in the junk drawer simply because your mother is hovering over your shoulder ("You never know when you're going to need that" and "Waste not, want not," she is saying), things like rubberbands, push pins, and pens with no tops. Also pennies, emery boards, and pen tops that don't fit any of your topless pens.

There are worse things you could do with a weekend afternoon than going through your junk drawer, so long as you realize it's just busywork and you're not really going to accomplish anything. Like volunteer committees, certain government agencies, and most junior high school kids, the contents of a junk drawer actively resist control. You can clean it all out, sort through it, and even throw a lot of it away, but you'll never really impose order on it.

So go ahead if you have nothing better to do with a few hours. Collect all the pennies and roll them in one of the coin wrappers. Check the date on each of the oatmeal coupons. Put the pink plaid shoelaces in your sneakers.

Test the batteries with your battery tester. Return the Monopoly tokens to the game box and flush the pills. (But save a few of the prescription vials. You never know when you're going to need one.)

Eat the Lifesavers. Fold the bread bags. Tie all the twist ties together. Make neat little piles of emery boards, rubberbands, paper clips, and push pins, and try all the caps on all the pens if you must.

Admire the neat little piles for a few minutes if you like. Then dump everything back in the drawer, uncork some Bully Hill, and go watch "Muscle Magazine" on ESPN. Acceptance is the key to better mental health. The stuff in a junk drawer is impossible to organize. If it weren't, it wouldn't be there.

Lost, and Found

IN the news today is yet another report on the lost chord. The elusive harmony was heard halfway through the second chorus of "Stouthearted Men" at today's luncheon meeting of the Pittsburgh Rotary Club (Midtown chapter). Thought until just recently to be extinct or severely diminished, the chord has been heard with increasing frequency during the past few months.

After years of silence, the chord surfaced September 9 in a junior high school band room in Pine Bluff, Arkansas, much to the surprise of Jimmy Siburski, an eighth grader in the trombone section. It was next heard in the choir loft of a small Methodist church in East Orange, New Jersey, during the regular Thursday evening rehearsal. It alighted among the tenors for a brief interval but almost before anyone recognized it, it was gone. Just last week the chord was heard again at Mildred Fitzler's sixty-third birthday party in Archbold, Ohio, outside of Toledo, about the time her neighbor, Lila Weston, began singing "How Old Are You?"

For years it was assumed that the chord migrated, spending its summers in a high school music camp near Cleveland and wintering somewhere in the vicinity of the St. Petersburg Singers. More recent data indicate that the chord's range has become augmented.

There are reports of the chord breeding in such diverse locations as open-mike clubs in New England college towns and community orchestra rehearsals in Arizona, where it often startles string players. George Handyside, a retired postal worker from

Ogalala, Nebraska, has been principal violist with the Sun City Seniors Philharmonic for nearly 11 years. "Someone really ought to band that little fellow," commented Handyside, 76, after a recent incident.

Illustrating remarkable adaptation to changing environmental factors, the chord has shown itself capable of survival in spite of an alarming increase of musical pollutants such as "lite" rock radio stations and Philip Glass. Some experts theorize that the chord has undergone a genetic mutation in response to the increasing decibel level of the contemporary soundscape, allowing it to achieve new dominance. The National Center for the Study of Acoustical Aberrations and Intervalic Phenomena in Bloomington, Indiana, has assigned a research team to study the matter.

Special lost chord bulletins have been issued to polka bands, barbershop quartets, and tenor saxophonists in 37 states. Meanwhile, groups of musicians across the country are urged to remain alert, regardless of their repertoire or instrumentation.

Festivities

Red, White, and Blue Monday

NOT too many years ago, we marked the birthdays of Lincoln and Washington individually, on February 12 and February 22, respectively. You could tell which was which by checking the bulletin board in your classroom: construction paper split-rail fences and tall black hats (flat ones, not to be confused with the pointy ones that go on the board with paper pumpkins in October) meant Lincoln's Birthday. Cherry trees with little hatchets buried in them meant Washington's Birthday. Although wooden teeth would have been more fun, the symbols were clear. There was never any doubt as to what was being celebrated.

Now, like a couple of beleaguered commuter airlines, these holidays have lost their identities to consolidation and merger. Many states still celebrate Lincoln's Birthday at its proper time, but since 1971, Washington's Birthday has been shoved around to create a three-day weekend. Now the third Monday in February, it's still called Washington's Birthday in most places (Washington Day in Arizona), though it seldom falls on the correct date. But in five states, one of them mine (the others are Pennsylvania, Colorado, Nebraska, and Hawaii, since you asked), it is decreed that this Monday holiday will be called Presidents' Day, a sort of all-purpose, generic tribute to our political icons.

Many schools are closed on Presidents' Day/Washington's Birthday. But some are not. You always have to check. To really confound things, some universities shift holiday observances back and forth between Mondays and Tuesdays like a moving target.

This is so that those classes meeting on Mondays won't end up short on instruction hours, but it pretty well undermines the long weekend idea, which was the whole reason for the holiday in the first place.

A few businesses are closed on Presidents' Day, but most are open, especially those at the mall, which is nice because it gives the kids who are out of school somewhere to go while their parents are at work. Whether the buses run on holiday schedule or make their usual weekday runs remains to be answered. Yes, it's a holiday, but most people have to go to work anyway. What do you think? And how about metered parking spaces that are free on Sundays and holidays? Does Presidents' Day count? (Tell *that* to the judge when you get a parking ticket.)

There are just two things you can be sure of. Neither mail nor money moves on Presidents' Day. Banks and post offices shut down for all holidays, including this one. Not only postal employees but all government workers (is that a contradiction in terms?) have the day off. As for those of us who labor in the private sector, a few are granted a day of leisure, but most have to go to work. Which is just as well, as we have no idea how we are to celebrate Presidents' Day anyway.

For example, should I be lucky enough to get Presidents' Day off, is it okay to use the time to clean the basement or catch up on some reading? Maybe I'm supposed to go to a parade or have some sort of a family dinner.

If we do have a Presidents' Day dinner, I wonder if there's anything in particular I should serve? We always have ham on Easter, turkey on Thanksgiving, and pork with sauerkraut for New Year's. Maybe we should have waffles for Presidents' Day. After all, presidents are politicians first. Come to think of it, either ham or turkey would be more than appropriate. Or even pork, served in a barrel, perhaps.

When we're done with dinner we could all stretch out on the floor in front of the hearth and read some history lessons by firelight. (Those whose homes lack real woodburners might substitute small electric space heaters.) And after the children are nestled all snug in their beds, maybe the Father of Our Country will slip down the chimney and leave Presidents' Day gifts for us, although if he does, we'll probably be required to donate them to the Smithsonian. I don't suppose it would be considered ethical to keep them.

I do hope our house (excuse me, I mean home) isn't supposed to be decorated in any way for Presidents' Day. I usually don't get around to taking down the Christmas lights until at least the end of January, and I really don't have time for any more of that sort of thing. Perhaps we could just hang a small hatchet from the chokecherry out by the split-rail fence, sing "Bewitched, Bothered and Bewildered," and let it go at that.

The No-Fault Valentine

TEDDY bears are soft, fuzzy persons who look like bears. Most of them are brown. Teddy bears tend to be plump, but they seldom go bald. Only a few of them need glasses, and then just for reading. Teddy bears are often very short, but they are not sensitive about it.

Teddy bears are handy to have around when you want someone to hug, and, if you're looking for a valentine, they are vastly superior to humans.

Teddy bears are always pleasant. They never argue or say "I told you so." Teddy bears don't read your mail. They don't lose phone messages or say rude things about your friends.

Teddy bears like to watch the very same TV shows as you. Teddy bears never criticize your taste in music. Teddy bears keep quiet when you're trying to read, and they let you lead when you dance.

Teddy bears don't sing in the shower. Neither do they snore. Teddy bears don't ask you to spend Sunday afternoon visiting their mother, and they always let you have the funnies first.

Teddy bears never complain about having cottage cheese for dinner five nights in a row because you're on a diet. They don't notice when your face breaks out, and they won't laugh at you when you're doing your exercises. Teddy bears don't discuss cellulite or complain about their sinuses, and they never have headaches.

Teddy bears won't exchange your Christmas presents, even if you buy the wrong size. They always let you choose the movie, but they won't blame you when it's not as good as the reviewer said it was.

Teddy bears never take the last chocolate-chip cookie on the plate. Teddy bears don't criticize your driving or correct your grammar.

Teddy bears don't complain if you forget to clean the tub, and they don't care if you leave the towels on the floor. Teddy bears never argue about whose turn it is to do the dishes.

Teddy bears don't yell at you when you can't make up your mind. Teddy bears never ask where you've been, and they don't get angry no matter how late you come home.

Teddy bears love you no matter *what* you do.

Eggsistential Experiences

EASTER eggs are not all they're cracked up to be. We're not talking, of course, about those exquisite little works of art created by Ukrainians with seemingly inexhaustible patience and all the proper equipment. We're talking about those blotchy and multi-colored symbols of new life whose creation leaves a rainbow of stains on your kitchen counter that won't come off even if you scrub them with straight bleach.

Face it. Not all Easter eggs are beautiful, unless you're a beholder with a real inside track. In fact, unless you've got a live-in Ukrainian at your house (excuse me, I mean home), most Easter eggs are not even within spitting distance of attractive.

Each year you get at least one mud-colored egg made by a prepubescent Future Scientist of America who just had to find out if red, yellow, and blue mixed together really do make brown. (They do. Trust me on this one.) And the grape-colored egg with a white oval on its side? That's the one that sat, untended, in a cup of purple dye for three hours. It was left behind by the preschooler who got bored with egg dyeing after four minutes and went in to watch "Muppet Babies."

Easter egg coloring kits provide all sorts of things to make your eggs interesting and attractive, including wax crayons with which to draw intricate designs on the shells. The intent is to prevent the dye from reaching that portion of the shell to which wax is applied, yielding a lovely design. It's a resist technique, sort of hard-boiled batik.

Of course, it doesn't work. If the dye water is hot enough to give you a half-way decent color, it's hot enough to melt the wax off the egg. If, indeed, all the wax were to melt off, the egg wouldn't look so bad, but only about 60 percent of it floats off. Your egg ends up looking like an acne sufferer who has just undergone a partial face peel.

The tissue-paper transfers (you know, the ones the kids end up applying to each other's foreheads) are another bust. They reproduce buck-toothed bunny faces with great clarity on the smooth surfaces of kitchen appliances, but always turn out blurry on the eggs.

Slightly more successful are the paper bunny ears and circular cardboard collars with little bow ties printed on them. However, the glue that's on their backside gives them about as much tenacity as an over-aged Green Stamp. To keep them from sliding off, you need to add your own adhesive, and for the truly creative child this can add a whole new dimension of fun to the egg-coloring activity. By the time your second grader has glued his middle finger (dyed blue) to the end of his nose, the thought of Easter eggs brings tears of deep regret to your eyes. But it isn't over.

In a few days, having been created, hidden, and, for the most part, found, your Easter eggs will have to be eaten. (Oh, yes, they will. "It's a sin to waste good food; there are children starving in China, etc."—Mothertape No. 371.) Those in prime condition go relatively quickly as deviled eggs. A little Miracle Whip (low-fat is alright), some dried mustard, maybe a dash of Worcestershire—you know how to do this—and most of your family will eat them.

Those in the next wave metamorphose into egg salad sandwiches for school lunches which no one eats. They are left in lockers to be rediscovered in June, perfuming the air with *eau de chemistry lab.*

If you're really ready for some peace and quiet, serve your family creamed curried eggs au gratin. For three nights thereafter your spouse will call to say that he has to work late ("Don't hold dinner, honey. I'll just grab a sandwich."), and each of your children beyond the age of six will wrangle an invitation to "eat over" at a friend's house.

No matter how hard you try to use up the Easter eggs, many clearly will have rounded the corner of inedibility before you can get to them in a culinary fashion. For those, you must find other uses. (Oh, yes, you must. "Waste not, want not"—Mothertape No. 7.)

You could take up juggling as a hobby, or crochet five or six eggs together to make a colorful doorstop whose fumes will drive the moths out of your front hall carpet.

Or . . . you might try splitting the eggs in half, hollowing them out, and using them as containers for your pantyhose. Sure, it sounds bizarre, but who knows? It just might catch on.

That's Entertainment?

WHEN I hear someone say "We're entertaining tonight," I immediately find myself wondering if the speaker means that she and her partner are dull and boring at other times. Or if perhaps they've gone into vaudeville. Maybe they wear tap shoes and carry shiny black canes.

Of course, I know what they really mean. They mean that they're having guests in for dinner.

I can handle that. Having people in for dinner can be fun, especially if they're people you really like. In fact, even if they're people you don't really like, having anybody in for dinner beats the heck out of spending the evening discussing post-Expressionist German art with your tropical fish.

Having people in for dinner is also a lot more fun than eating microwavable "Gourmet a Go-go" in front of MacNeil/Lehrer, and it gives you an excuse to cook something like stuffed grape leaves or Chinese smoked chicken that you probably wouldn't bother to make just for yourself. But entertaining?

You can have friends in for dinner any time the mood strikes, but to entertain you have to clean your house (excuse me, I mean home). You can pitch a party on a moment's notice, provided you can muster a minyan of like-minded friends and it's not too late to order pizza, but to entertain you have to plan for weeks.

Entertaining requires matching stemware and a full set of unchipped china. If you're having a few friends in for dinner it's enough to clear the newspaper clippings and unopened mail off the dining room table. To entertain you need candles and a cunning centerpiece, color-coordinated with your unchipped china.

To entertain you need an elegant hostess gown or at least some of those Hollywood-at-home pajamas, the ones with the big, wide legs. When you're just having friends in for dinner you can wear your sweat pants and Reeboks or whatever it is that your friends normally have to look at you in.

If you're just having some friends in for dinner, everyone will be perfectly happy with appetizers or even some munchies, but if you're entertaining you'll need to make hors d'oeuvres.

It's a problem of connotation more than anything. Aside from the Fred Astaire image that it conjures up, the word "entertaining" is anxiety producing.

Entertaining requires that you prepare "dishes," clever preparations that take days to make and call for ingredients costing a week's salary and available only at a specialty store on the other side of town, ingredients like pignolias, chanterelles, and asafetida powder. If you're merely having some friends in for dinner (make that supper—truth in advertising), it's okay just to cook some good food, using the sort of everyday stuff you already have in your kitchen.

If you're entertaining, your menu must be beautifully balanced and ethnically consistent, i.e., you can't serve hasenpfeffer and tortellini at the same dinner even though you may think they taste good together. You must have appropriate side dishes to complement the main dish and, even more difficult, a dessert that isn't Häagen-Dazs out of the carton.

Non-dinner entertaining is just as intimidating. I'll put the kettle on if anyone stops by in the late afternoon (for sweets we can always make cinnamon toast if Girl Scout cookies aren't in season), but entertaining with a tea is completely out of the question. To give a tea your china and centerpiece must be not only unchipped and cunning, respectively, but charming as well. And probably pink. I don't know about you, but I've never owned any pink china, and it wouldn't be wise to hold your breath.

Also, I'm certain Amy Vanderbilt or Miss Manners or someone has decreed that you must wear a hat when you pour. Except for the one I wear when I go skiing I don't own a hat either. Even if I did, I think a hat would look silly with my sweat pants and Reeboks, don't you?

A luncheon? That speaks of white gloves, equally silly with sweat pants and Reeboks. A sophisticated little backyard picnic? If God had really meant for us to eat outdoors, flies and ants would never have been created. As for entertaining with a brunch, the only good reason to do so is that it lends social acceptability to drinking Bloody Marys before noon. (That may be reason enough. We could pick up a bag of sausage biscuits . . .)

So come over for dinner (excuse me, I mean supper) anytime. You can even bring a friend. I'll move the newspaper clippings aside and serve you some good food on a plate that may or may not be chipped but definitely won't be pink. Maybe we'll even have appetizers first, but don't expect me to entertain. Unless, of course, I answer the door wearing my tap shoes instead of Reeboks.

Dear Dad,

IT isn't that I didn't try. I did. Really, I did. I looked. I read the ads. I pounded the pavement. I marched the mall. I shopped till I dropped. But I just couldn't find the right thing.

There's this guy on Channel 19 who thinks I should buy you a Garden Weasel, the miracle five-in-one garden tool that tills, weeds, cultivates, aerates, and I can't think of the fifth thing, only $19.99 at your True Value Hardware store, the perfect gift for Dad.

He's right. It would be perfect, if you needed it. He means well, I think. He just hasn't considered the fact that a guy in his seventies who's been gardening practically since the close of the Bronze Age already has all the tools he needs.

Also on Channel 19 is an older fellow who isn't Art Linkletter but could be who says the perfect gift for Father's Day is this lounge chair that adjusts to nine different positions and has its own built-in foot rest and a patented head and neck support to give you individualized comfort. Pretty neat, huh?

Maybe I should buy both the Garden Weasel and the lounge chair. After you've weaseled your garden those four different ways plus the one I can't think of, you could spend the evening experimenting with the nine positions on the chair. (I could charge it . . . MasterCard and Visa are accepted.)

Handy Andy's "Great Gifts for Dad" (not perfect, mind you, but still great) include a steel-cradle hammer holder and a deluxe carpenter construction apron. Speaking of aprons, how about a barbeque apron that reads "Caution: Man Cooking"? It comes with a matching chef's toque. There's also the Stanley 12-inch maple miter box. You could whip out a couple of hats for the bishop in your wood shop . . .

Another thing that caught my eye was a rechargeable Krypton flashlight, on sale for $11.99, only $9.99 after rebate. (I wouldn't even need to charge that. I could pay cash.) Seventy percent brighter than an ordinary flashlight, rugged plastic with a no-slip grip, weather resistant, shock resistant, able to light tall buildings with a single beam.

Sears' Father's Day Sale (actually it's the Sears' Six Days Before Father's Day Sale, but they're not calling it that) is featuring oxford-cloth summer-weight dress shirts (pink, mint green, and yellow—sorry, no blue) and Sun Bay beach-inspired separates for Dad. Could you use a pair of surfer shorts? How about a pink oxford-cloth summer-weight dress shirt? I read somewhere that men who wear pink shirts are totally secure in their masculinity. And I could charge it.

K-Mart's "Great Gift Ideas for Dad" (not perfect gifts, not great gifts, but great gift *ideas*) include the Whirlpool personal home spa. That might be fun. If I bought you that maybe you'd let me come over and use it. K-Mart has a lot of digital watches, too, presumably for fathers who haven't learned to tell time yet, and more surfer shorts. I think they also have some pink shirts. (I could charge it at K-Mart, too, but it's really kind of a hassle, you know, because you have to have all this identification and they take your picture and everything . . .)

I could have gotten you an electronic musical keyboard (now there's a contradiction) or a digital world-time travel alarm clock (so you could not tell time anywhere in the world and still get up), just two of Radio Shack's "Perfect Gifts for Grads and Dads." I hope you don't mind sharing. Or how about headrest speakers for your car? Velcro fasteners make them easier to install and air suspension woofers give you crisp sound. They have in-line splice connectors, too, whatever those are. Of course, you'll have to get a tape deck, or at least a radio, put in the station wagon.

Although it isn't suggested specifically for Father's Day, I could get you a model of a human skeleton from the Smithsonian. The catalog says you can learn the name of every bone in your body as you put together your very own six-foot skeleton. (Your very own skeleton that you've had as long as I've known you is more like 5′10″. Does this mean you'll be taller after you finish the job?) Sturdy pre-cut poster board pieces, number coded for easy assembly. ("The 48's connected to the [clap] 60. The 60's connected to the [clap] 15 . . .") You could have a lot of fun with this. Mom could accompany you on the electronic musical keyboard.

How about a 100-percent-cotton terry-cloth 32″-by-70″ custom-embroidered bath sheet that says "Big Daddy" on it? I mean, at 5′10″ you may not be NBA material, but height alone does not a big dad make. And the towel does come in blue.

Then there's the battery-powered planetarium that lights up the ceiling with 31 constellations at once. It comes with a bunch of stuff—master projection disc, replaceable bulb, guide to position the North Star for your area, star-finder chart, etc. (Batteries not included, but I can charge it.) You could lie on your back in one of those nine positions and pick out the Pleiades on your living room ceiling. That may not be perfect, but doesn't it sound great? (Maybe Mom could manage a little electronic Hoagy Carmichael . . .)

Besides all this great and perfect stuff, I found some "Terrific Gifts for Dad" and a few "Wonderful Gifts for Dad." I also found "Gifts for Great Dads" and "Gifts to Make Dad's Day." I even ran across a thing or two "For the Man Who Has Everything." (I'm sure I remember him. Didn't he used to belong to your Kiwanis Club?)

Nobody, however, seems to be selling "Pretty Good Gifts" or "Okay Gifts." And no one is hyping gifts—perfect, great, pretty good, or otherwise—for the man who *doesn't* have everything. And doesn't want it!

Imagine! My very own 5′10″ blue-shirted, time-telling father, my non-surfer-short-wearing, tool-rich gardening dad of dads, is in the vanguard, a member of the only demographic segment in our society as yet untargeted by modern marketing efforts. I never realized until now how statistically significant you are, but then, I suppose none of us ever really appreciates our parents until we're adults ourselves.

Anyway, Happy Father's Day, Dad. And be sure to let me know if you change your mind about the pink shirt.

Love,

Your Daughter

P.S. I could charge it . . .

Stuff the Turkey

I KNOW what you're having for dinner the fourth Thursday in November. And you know what I'm having. I wouldn't dare serve anything else, and neither would you. Especially if you have children. Once they latch onto something, children, for all the good press accorded youth, are the most inflexible, hidebound traditionalists around.

Order pizza two busy Fridays in a row and you will ever after hear, "but we *always* have pizza on Friday." Make a rainbow cake with candy flowers on the icing for your four-year-old's birthday and you will be stuck making it every year until she is at least 23, because "you *always* make rainbow cake with candy flowers on the icing for my birthday."

This of course doesn't work with any food that is ordinary, nutritious, or economical. Cook something like that for dinner and you'll hear "we *never* have anything good," meaning it's been two days since you've ordered pizza.

But you can't order pizza on Thanksgiving, and even if you could, your kids would insist on turkey because (all together now) "we *always* have turkey on Thanksgiving."

Magazine and newspaper food articles from time to time humorously suggest that we break out of our rut and serve goose with lingonberries, duck bigarade, or even (gasp!) roast beef. Don't try it. These features are written by people who either have no families or are from another planet. Here on earth, in the good old US of A, our reactionary children would never permit such radical departures from tradition.

Not only is the main course completely unalterable, we are also restrained by these young Tories from changing or omitting any of the side dishes or accompaniments. Take the matter of stuffing, for example.

A "blended" family I know nearly came to blows one year when the resident stepmother packed the turkey with the sage-and-onion bread stuffing she and her kids traditionally have. His children consider cornbread dressing absolutely essential.

I once threw some chopped apples in our turkey stuffing—don't ask me why. Thank goodness it wasn't much work and I rather liked the way it tasted, because I've been forced to do it every year since. As far as my offspring are concerned, turkey dressing isn't turkey dressing unless it has chopped apples in it.

You can't be too careful, though. Break down once and top your sweet potatoes with miniature marshmallows and you're doomed. Cut the jellied cranberry sauce into little turkey shapes with a cookie cutter and you'll be doing it for at least a decade.

Near as I can tell, no one really eats cranberry sauce anyway. The lumpy kind with the skins and seeds in it spends the dinner being passed from hand to hand unconsumed, and the jellied stuff mostly slides off onto the tablecloth, regardless of whether it's been cut into little turkey shapes or not. But we have to have it because (you know) "we always have cranberry sauce on Thanksgiving."

I could tell you that they grow out of it, but I wouldn't want to raise any false hopes. Last Thanksgiving seated with me around my table were just two friends of modest proportions and one full-sized son who is as grown as he is going to be.

On a scale from mild masochism to sheer lunacy, the idea of cooking a turkey for only four people struck me as falling somewhere around "cruel and unusual self-punishment." Instead of getting up at seven in the morning to wrestle a slippery, naked bird into the oven, I baked four, manageable little Cornish hens. They were cleverly accompanied by wild rice and mushrooms, green beans, and a nice salad.

It was a cook's dream. No mixing stuffing in a washtub, no inevitably leftover sweet potatoes with all the miniature marshmallows picked off the top, no cranberry jelly sliding onto the tablecloth. Just a nice meal.

Son, who comes with an appetite and shoe size that are a matched set, chowed down, as they say. He ate his Cornish hen plus half of mine, and made quite sure that we wouldn't have to deal with any leftover beans or rice.

Later, after downing two pieces of pie, he stood in the dining room inhaling the last bits of salad from the serving bowl. I asked him how he liked dinner. "Well," he said, "it was okay. But it didn't seem like Thanksgiving. I mean, we always have *turkey* on Thanksgiving."

I should have ordered pizza.

Giving by Number

WHEN your children are very small, Christmas shopping is lots of fun. Give a preschooler a three-dollar flashlight and she'll play with it for a month. A set of colored markers is received as a treasure worthy of display in the British Museum, and a small, generic stuffed animal becomes a 24-hour buddy.

By the time they reach second grade, though, most kids have been infected with the virulent consumer virus spread by television and take to enumerating their demands in highly brand-specific terms. The only items these kids can be convinced to play with are ridiculously expensive and as scarce as fast food in Moscow, leading to the sorry spectacle of otherwise proud Americans queuing up to spend half a week's salary on a toy that will be broken or discarded within a day.

Adolescents want all manner of clothes, records, and other paraphernalia, and some of it even falls within your price range. But in the time it takes you to buy it, drive home, and wrap it, whatever it is goes out of style and they don't want it anymore. As for adults, some people, like your parents or grandparents, really do have everything and they don't want any more of it. Others, perhaps your aunt and uncle, have a wish list, but there's nothing on it you can consider buying unless you knock off a Brink's truck first.

One semisolution to the gift-giving dilemma is the gift exchange. You know how it works—each person draws a name and is responsible for selecting a gift for that person. Under this system, everybody both gives and gets one gift.

If you like, you can carry the gift exchange idea a step further and simply name a Designated Present Receiver for your family. All the gifts, no matter what they are or for whom they were purchased, go to that one person. The others can simply enjoy the thoughts of the givers, which, after all, are what count, right?

Since it is the thought that counts, there may be no reason to exchange real gifts at all. Instead, why not exchange pictures of gifts? The Sears catalog has a nice selection. This could save you tons of money and allows you much more freedom of expression than when you give real gifts.

For example, if you're only cutting pictures out of the Sears catalog, why not give your Great-aunt Mildred an Arnold Schwarzenegger weight-lifting bench, something you'd never give her if you were giving real gifts. Give your mother a sump pump or a gasoline-powered chain saw. Cut out a Winnie-the-Pooh baby crib for your obnoxious eleven-year-old brother.

Use your imagination. Give your father a pair of orthopedic shoes and a nursing bra. And for the teenager in the family, consider pictures of his very own leaf rake and snow shovel. Those never go out of style.

To stray even further into the abstract, you might assign numbers to the 50 most commonly exchanged gifts. For example, agree that a tie is a 23. A gift box of bath powder is a 45. Mittens or gloves are a 17, a silk scarf is a 33, and a book from the best-seller list is a 14 in hardbound, a 9 in paperback.

Now, instead of buying any presents or bothering with cutting out pictures of gifts, just print the number of the gift you were thinking of giving on a three-by-five index card. Seal it in an envelope—decorated if you're so inclined—and put it under the tree.

An additional benefit of this plan is that you can fit scads of presents under the tree. One size fits all and they're a snap to exchange. If you don't like your gift, you just cross out the number and write another.

Besides, it's the thought that counts. Right?

Santaclaustrophobia

IT'S Christmas Eve. . . . Do you know where your lawyer is?

Ponder this: the man who would become Santa Claus was born in the fourth century A.D. Nearly 1700 years old and he's running around on rooftops! Given December weather in most of the country, there's a fair chance things will be wet or even icy overhead. What if this fat, old elf slips? On your roof?

In our litigious society, *santaclaustrophobia*—clinically defined as a persistent fear of fat, bearded elves climbing down your chimney—can no longer be considered neurotic. Sure, climbing around on slippery rooftops obviously qualifies as reckless behavior for someone of Santa's age, but is that enough to relieve you of liability? Or have you shirked your responsibility as a property owner by not getting out on the roof and spreading rock salt around?

What if Santa falls, slides down your roof, and catches himself on the gutter, the one running the length of the front porch, the one that you know is loose but haven't gotten around to fixing yet? Properly repaired, that gutter might have broken Santa's fall and prevented an injury. In this case, your negligence is clear.

And don't let his jolly demeanor or the fact that he started out as a bishop working the territory around Turkey fool you into thinking that Santa won't sue. All it would take is for some sleigh-chasing legal eagle to start filling him with the idea that he "deserves" compensation for this terrible mishap, and you'd be cooked. There's not a court in the land that would rule against Santa Claus.

You can't be too careful. Suppose your minor child (with your knowledge and consent) writes a letter to Santa requesting specific gift items, and Santa is thwarted in his attempt to deliver those gifts because you forgot to leave the damper open. Have you broken a contract?

What if this fat elf gets stuck in your chimney? Say the opening from the flue into your fireplace is just too small to accommodate a 300-pound elf. Are you required by law to alter your chimney to make it accessible to all elves, regardless of their size? Does failure to do so make you ineligible for federal chimney grant funds? Must you provide a designated handicapped sleigh-parking place on your roof?

Then there's always the chance that Santa will develop lung cancer twenty years from now due to the accumulated carcinogens in your flue. Sure, you called the chimney sweep, but because you procrastinated until late September the chimney sweep couldn't give you an appointment. The only time he had was during the last week of October, the same week you were going to be at a conference in Honolulu.

Maybe the liability is the chimney sweep's because, although he knew a dangerous situation existed, he didn't alter his schedule to rectify it. After all, he should be able to understand that you had no choice but to go to the conference in Honolulu. Skipping the conference could mean your job and if you lost your job you would have been unable to pay the chimney sweep for his services.

How about those cholesterol-laden butter cookies you leave on the fireplace for Santa every year? Aren't you contributing to his risk of heart disease? He's obviously a prime candidate: male, drastically overweight, and under a tremendous amount of stress with the kind of deadlines he has to meet.

It might be best just to cover yourself and slap a warning label on those cookies. "Caution: these cookies contain saturated fat and may contribute to a greater risk of heart disease in plump elves." You should probably list the sugar and sodium contents as well, since the overweight are more likely to develop diabetes and high blood pressure, too.

Even though it's traditional, do you really want a 300-pound, 1700-year-old elf trotting around on your roof and shimmying down your chimney? You may want to check your neighborhood hardware store for a "Santa Guard" to put over your chimney. It's a wire affair not unlike those designed to keep raccoons from nesting in your flue. While you're there, pick up a can of "Santa-No" or some other nontoxic elf repellent to spray on your roof. As a backup, you could lightly electrify the perimeter of your chimney so that it delivers a noticeable but harmless shock to the old guy.

Santa isn't the only possible plaintiff you could come up against. Legal dangers lurk in all crevices of this insidious holiday. Say, for example, you buy a nice, shiny red wagon for your three-year-old son. It comes in a box (some assembly required), and so Christmas Eve you spread all the parts out on the living room floor and do your best to put the thing together. It looks okay, and you only have a couple of little nuts and bolts left over, but the first time your son tries to ride in the wagon a wheel falls off, the wagon tips over, and your son hits his head on the sidewalk and sustains a brain concussion.

Fourteen years later this same kid is denied a scholarship to the expensive Ivy League college of his choice because his SAT scores are not quite high enough. You can't afford to send him there without that financial aid, and he has to go to a state school instead. When he graduates, he can't find a job that will pay him the kind of starting salary he had in mind. The kid sues you, his parent, claiming that the injury he sustained because of your inept assembly of the wagon prevented him from taking full advantage of his early educational opportunities and will severely limit his lifetime earning capabilities.

Your defense is that, after all, anybody could make a mistake, especially when the directions seem to have been written in English by someone who only speaks Korean. And you're not really very mechanically inclined anyway, maybe because shop wasn't on your class schedule in eighth grade since you played trombone and band practice was the same period as shop class.

So who's liable here? You, for misassembling the wagon? The manufacturer, for not providing directions that even a trombone player who never took shop in the eighth grade could handle? The guidance counselor, for approving your class schedule even though shop wasn't on it? The band director? Your trombone teacher?

Your mother, for buying the trombone in the first place? Or the music store that sold your mother the trombone?

Unless you have time to watch all the reruns of *The Paper Chase*, the only way to deal with these questions is to retain an attorney who specializes in holiday law. But it's probably cheaper to spend the last half of December in some nice, warm Moslem country and just skip the whole Christmas thing.

Keeping the World Safe
for Singing

WELL, of course, there are some people who can't sing. Though perfectly normal in other respects, and frequently of average or better intelligence, for whatever reason, these poor unfortunates are unable to carry a tune around the corner.

It's usually not even their fault. Perhaps their mothers took drugs during pregnancy or listened to too much top-40 radio. We don't blame them, and we do the best we can to include them in the activities of the singing world.

In fact, it's always nice to have a nonsinger along, for example, when you go to the old ball game. That way there's someone to go buy you some peanuts and Crackerjacks while you're singing the national anthem.

For college football games it's fairly simple to pass your non-singer off as an alumnus of another school who is just unfamiliar with the alma mater. And at Rotary Club luncheons, nonsingers are often chosen to hand out the song sheets. This keeps them busy through at least two choruses of "Stouthearted Men" without calling attention to their handicap.

Never hesitate to invite a nonsinger to your New Year's Eve party for fear your other guests will find it awkward. By putting the nonsinger in charge of the streamers or sending her off in search of another corkscrew, there's a chance you can maintain a mellifluous *auld lang syne*. But if not, you can assume that even your friends with perfect pitch will be sufficiently lubricated to enjoy the resultant polytonality.

On the other hand, the insipid little waltz that we warble at birthday parties doesn't sound all that great even without a nonsinger gumming up the harmonic works. Until the candles are extinguished, the best place for a nonsinger at a birthday party is behind the camera . . . even if there's no film in it.

Of course, I'm not suggesting that nonsingers be prevented from singing in public if they really want to. It's a free country, and people who wish to embarrass themselves will always find a way.

For the most part, nonsingers have been successfully mainstreamed into society. We even welcome them to our church services. The door is always open. (Nonsingers' entrance is around the back, on the ground floor, to the left of the boiler room.)

Although some congregations, especially the Methodists, prefer to maintain separate seating for nonsingers, that probably isn't necessary. Usually a written pledge to the effect that they will refrain from droning the Doxology is sufficient.

As for the Christmas Eve carol service, nonsingers can always arrange to be in Florida that week.

Strictly Personal

Thirty-Something Else

BEING over 30 (alright . . . over 40) is not the lamentable position it's sometimes held out to be. (Of course it probably means you won't be competing in the next Olympic games, but at least you won't have to spend any time training. Aging is something you can do perfectly well without a coach. And no special equipment is required.)

When we were younger there were more of us than there were of them. The median age of the population was under 25 and we didn't trust anybody over 30. Now, the median age of the population is past the 30-year mark, and so are we, and by 1990, there were more adult women over 40 than under. It's good to be grown up, and those of us on the far side of the milestones, while reluctantly bidding farewell to unlined faces and flat stomachs, have a lot going for us.

First of all, there are still more of us than there are of them, just like there were when we were them and our parents were us. Furthermore, there are fewer and fewer of them every year, which means that pretty soon it should be easier to get a parking space at the mall.

Even though there are more of us than there are of them, we make more money than they do. Some experts say we also make more money than they will when they get to be us, although some of us make less in real dollars than our parents did when they were us.

Younger Americans are more susceptible to some of the new flu viruses that from time to time make their way over from Asia. People under 30 who were never exposed to the highly virulent viruses that circulated in the fifties and sixties are at particular risk. I read that in the Tuesday health section of the daily newspaper, which more of us than them read on a regular basis.

The under-30s may have more hair than we do but they also have more acne. And they obviously have less taste. For proof (of their level of taste, not their acne) listen first to a Cleveland Orchestra recording of any Mozart symphony; then listen to the latest rap or heavy metal hit. And fashion sense? Okay, so they've got good bodies, but just look at some of the stuff they deck those bodies in.

The disparity is obvious. Our superior taste is probably due to the many cultural advantages we enjoyed while growing up. We had Rocky and Bullwinkle; they had Speed Racer. We read *Mad Magazine* and listened to symphonic music (in the background of Bugs Bunny cartoons). They don't read anything and they listen to MTV.

If you're over 35, you're too old to join the army, good news for somebody out there, I'm sure. And, speaking just to my fellow females, if you're over 35, you're probably finished producing babies. (I'll let you rate the good news quotient on that one yourself.)

They get more cavities than we do, and it couldn't happen to a nicer age group. After 25, says my dentist, the incidence of tooth decay decreases dramatically. It's nice to think of all of them, with their unlined faces and their flat stomachs, spending the afternoon at the dentist's. This also should help the parking situation at the mall.

Younger people move more often than we do, and as far as I'm concerned they deserve it. We read more books and go to more concerts than they do and, if you don't count fast-food restaurants (I don't), we eat out more than they do.

Our chances of being murdered are much lower than theirs, especially if we are female, which I, in this case, am very glad to be. Their car insurance rates are also much higher, but their standardized test scores are not by a long shot.

As for how they do at Scrabble, no statistics are available. But I'd be willing to bet we've got them there, too.

Where I Live

I DON'T live anywhere. I used to live somewhere, but I moved, and where I live now isn't anyplace at all. It doesn't have a name. It's just a house (excuse me, you know I mean a home), on a street, with a number. That's all.

The condominium where I used to live (in Rocky River, Ohio, since you asked) is one of a group known collectively as Golden Oaks, although I can't tell you why. There were no oaks, golden or otherwise, anywhere on the grounds. Just a few small crab apples near my balcony and a couple of locust trees in the back.

Not far from Golden Oaks is a smaller group of condos called Riverbank Estates. They're nice enough, I suppose, although I think calling them estates is stretching things a little, and they're at least three miles from the nearest river. As for banks, well, the closest ones are at the mall, and those are only branch offices.

One of my friends used to live in a place called the Courtyard, which, near as I can remember, didn't have a courtyard. In fact, I don't think it had any yard at all, but that's one of the things many people like about living in a condominium or an apartment. No yard, no yard work. Still, it doesn't go very far toward explaining the name.

There probably hasn't been a quail at Quail Hollow since the first bulldozer lumbered in. Ditto for the wildlife at Whitetail Run, Fawn Lake, and the Sandpiper. I won't venture such a statement about Big Turtle Apartments, "big" being a relative term and therefore, like a wet turtle, a little slippery, but I'd bet the farm that neither Eagle's Point nor Pheasant's Walk sports the species it's named for. And let's not even discuss Bear Creek. I mean, bears in Cleveland, Ohio? Chicago, maybe, but not Cleveland.

As for the Woodhawk development, an upscale planned-community-type operation on the east side of town that includes apartments, town houses, cluster homes, and detached dwellings, it's named for a nonexistent raptor. Roger Tory Peterson's *A Field Guide to the Birds East of the Rockies* (a definitive work—ask any birder) lists no such hawk. Neither does *The Birder's Handbook* or Golden Press's *Birds of North America* (a decent guide but not, in my opinion, on a par with Peterson). You'd think with all the money they're pouring into that place they could afford to name it for a real bird.

There may be a kernel of truth in the names of Walnut Hill (just one hill) and Hickory Hills (more than one hill), but if Chestnut Lake has any chestnuts, you can bet they're imported, probably from Italy. Orchard Hill (also only one hill) and MacIntosh Farms may have apple trees, but I feel certain there's no citrus anywhere in Orange Tree Estates except in the residents' refrigerators. Orange trees are even more unlikely in northeast Ohio than bears.

One of the few real estate entities that has any sense to its name is the Riverbend Condominiums. This one is downtown in a part of Cleveland known as the Flats and it's right on the Cuyahoga River, which means, by the way, "Crooked River." Purchase one of these units on the Cuyahoga and if you forget where you live, you know where to look for your house. You just have to remember which bend in the crooked river. In most cases, though, this kind of logic will get you into trouble.

Churchill Downs sounds as if it should be in Kentucky, but it's right here in northeast Ohio. North Church Towers ought to be in Boston, but it's here too. So are Nantucket Cove, which ought to be off the coast of mainland Massachusetts, and Walden, which also belongs in Massachusetts. As for the Alamo Apartments, they're only about ten miles south of my place. Even my grasp of geography is better than that.

It gets sillier. The nearby Village in the Park is neither a village nor a park. It's a building with a road on one side and a parking lot on the other. And the Islander isn't in the East Indies or the South Seas. It's an apartment complex on the west side of Cleveland, surrounded on all sides by pavement.

Of course, more truthful names might not do much for occupancy or sales. Interstate Estates and Concrete Hill lack the cachet of more bucolic monikers. Suburban Towers and Fast Food Ridge, for all their accuracy, wouldn't have much appeal, although I kind of like the idea of Mallview. (On a clear day, you can see a parking space . . .)

If where I live were a development instead of just a block of homes, it might be called Railview, since my home is near the tracks (on the right side, of course). Shortstop Hollow is another possibility, since the ballfield is just beyond the train tracks. Or Big Squirrel Homes (not houses, homes). That has a nice ring to it and would be very appropriate, given the neighborhood's healthy population of bushytailed rodents, fed fat on the acorns of our many nongolden oaks.

My favorite thought, though, is something like "Village in the City" or "City in the Town," because it doesn't really tell you a thing. Just like street names and house numbers. They convey no atmosphere, conjure up no particular ambiance. They don't tell anything at all about where you live. Except, of course, exactly where it is.

Virus-of-the-Month Club

LOOK, I know you've been sick. Of course, you have. Whatever it is, there's a lot of it going around. Everybody's been sick lately.

I know I certainly have been. In fact, I have reason to believe that someone—perhaps my weird niece in Indiana wishing to give me a truly unusual Christmas gift—signed me up for the Virus-of-the-Month Club.

"Twelve relatively mild but thoroughly annoying and untreatable infections, delivered automatically, one each month. Every selection guaranteed unique and sufficiently bothersome to completely disrupt the lucky recipient's work and leisure activities." (She probably fell for their advertising pitch: "Give the gift that keeps on giving." Too bad she didn't just cut out the ad and send me that. After all, it's the thought that counts.)

The January selection was a classic: runny nose, scratchy throat, sleep-disturbing cough, sneezing, slight fever. It arrived, gift wrapped, on New Year's Eve, approximately one hour before the stroke of midnight. It was a perfect beginning to the new year—nothing serious enough to send me to the doctor but more than sufficient to make me feel like the "before" shot in a Nyquil commercial for a week.

After that infection departed, I took a little time off to look after the important business of replenishing my supply of chicken soup and buying stock in Kimberly-Clark. I picked up an institutional size bottle of chewable vitamin C, bought a new sweat suit, and rented three videos. I was ready when, the morning of Ground Hog's Day, my February selection arrived. (I obviously had neglected to send back the card with an "X" in the little box next to "Send no selection this month.")

An interesting little virus, this one featured somewhat milder and less disgusting upper respiratory symptoms than the January selection, but with the nifty added twist of chills and some very intriguing dizziness. It kept me occupied right through Valentine's Day. This is probably just as well, as the chances of anything or anyone else keeping me occupied on Valentine's Day were unlikely, but that's another matter.

Although a fairly new member of the Virus-of-the-Month Club, apparently I already had accumulated some bonus points. While I'd not anticipated receiving my next virus until the beginning of March, another showed up hard on the heels (or whatever it is viruses have) of February's selection.

This one, according to the busy intake nurse at the very crowded drive-through clinic, appeared to be flu of the trendy Shanghai-A variety. Please don't misunderstand me. I'm not complaining, really. This latest bug is probably as close as I'll ever get to Shanghai or any other exotic port of call.

I'm not without appreciation for the romance of it all. A few years ago it was the Hong Kong flu, and I believe before that the season's most popular virus was from Alaska, another place I've never been. In fact, the most exotic place I've ever been is Russia, where they can't produce enough viruses for their own people, let alone enough to export. But while I've stayed home, my upper respiratory system has been around the Pacific Rim several times by association.

The Shanghai bug turned out to be quite similar to the January selection but, true to the Virus-of-the-Month Club's promise, had its own special qualities. I do think the bronchial congestion and secondary ear infection may have been something of a slip-up on the part of the selection committee, though. Both of those responded to medication, which made me wonder.

Now I'm confused. I've written to the club headquarters in Garden City, New Jersey, to inquire as to whether this last was indeed a bonus virus or merely the March selection sent a little early.

No answer has been forthcoming. Meanwhile, I'm looking into the possibility of canceling my club membership.

Or at least transferring it to somebody else.

It's Just That
I Have My Standards

I AM not a fussy eater. No, really—I'm not. (That woman in the back row, the one waving her arms and yelling "the kid's a liar," is my mother. Just try to ignore her.)

I offer as evidence the fact that I eat onions, mushrooms, and even liver, foods the truly fussy wouldn't dream of eating.

Liver, for example, can be quite attractive in the form of paté, though it's obviously inedible in any other guise. Onions are delicious sautéed in butter till golden or fried crispy. Limp fragments floating around in your soup looking like scraps of used gauze bandage are quite another matter.

When it comes to mushrooms, I'm extremely liberal. I enjoy them raw in salads and stuffed (crab meat is nice), broiled, or sautéed, so long as they've not been canned. While we're on the subject of tinned abominations, let me say that, of course, I eat green peas. Note that the operative word here is "green." Canned peas are not green; they are olive drab.

Generally speaking, I'm quite a fan of certain vegetables that fussy eaters are notorious for rejecting. I've always liked spinach, providing it, too, hasn't been canned, and wax beans are delicious fresh from the garden. I enjoy broccoli in moderation, and I'm fond of asparagus, although too few cooks realize that to be properly prepared it really should be peeled.

I won't touch anything with green peppers in it, but that has nothing to do with fussiness. I'm allergic to them. It's true, I also don't like them, but then you'd be hard pressed to develop much affection for something that makes the inside of your mouth swell up.

I do draw the line at vegetables that have spent substantial portions of their life cycle underground. Why would I want to eat a root that had to be dug up out of the dirt? Potatoes don't count. They're tubers, not roots.

Consider the usual selection of subterranean vegetables (in alphabetical order): beets, carrots, parsnips, and turnips. All are mundane to the utmost, with a glamour quotient and silhouette similar to that of your average Eastern-bloc factory worker.

Out of respect for Mel Blanc, I make an exception for carrots, and I sometimes eat beets if they're pickled, but I've never even been tempted to taste a turnip. As for parsnips, they're nothing less than a tragic waste of perfectly good photosynthesis.

I am every bit as open to various protein possibilities as I am to forms of produce. Eggs are more than acceptable, so long as they're not the least bit runny. I eat beef (medium rare), pork (well done), and lamb (slightly pink). Of course, these muscle meats must be served plain, as masking them with gravy or sauces impedes the necessary removal of every visible molecule of fat. (Could someone please help my mother back to her seat?)

And I love seafood. Fussy people don't eat seafood. I eat steamed clams and mussels, properly bearded. I like scallops (the little bay ones), shrimp (not fried), fresh (never frozen) sole, and perch (lake, not ocean).

Chicken is among my favorites, and, according to the American Heart Association, leaving the skin on your plate is a very healthy move. As for sushi . . . you'll forgive me, but a good friend of mine did her master's thesis on the liver fluke. Do you have any idea what percentage of people in Japan suffer from various intestinal parasites?

As a general rule, I do not eat or drink anything containing hot milk. That includes New England–style clam chowder, hot chocolate, and cream-of-anything. This I will admit to as a prejudice, but one that conveys a lot of common sense as it eliminates the possibility of either cream-style corn or creamed chipped beef ever turning up on the menu.

Really, I'm not fussy at all. (Mother, *please* stop sobbing.) It's just that I have my standards.

Beyond (Way Beyond) the Pale

FALL, as I write this, is here. And this year I'm ready for it. (Okay, it's only early September, but never mind this stuff about equinoxes and solstices. No matter what the calendar-makers say, we all know summer really begins on Memorial Day and ends Labor Day weekend.) I've cleaned the storm windows, signed up for my adult education class, and stocked up on Halloween candy. But most important, I've gotten a terrific head start on my winter pallor.

In past years I've gone into autumn with a fading summer tan that lingered for months, but this time I did it right. I stayed pale all summer, and I'm starting September with a beautiful pallor—smooth, even, all-over fish-belly white. No strap marks, no peeling, no golden-brown glow, not even a stray freckle. I mean, I am *really* pale.

In fact, to look at me you'd think I spent the entire summer at an ultra-expensive resort near San Francisco. You know, the sort of place where the beautiful people go to get pale: spa cuisine and guaranteed overcast 342 days a year. I'm so pale I look like I've just come back from a midwinter vacation in St. Paul, Minnesota, or at least a month in Gary, Indiana.

I know all my friends think I spent a fortune getting this pallor, but actually I never left Cleveland. This smooth ivory look didn't come from any paling parlor either. No, indeed. I got this beautiful healthy-looking pallor in my spare time, right in my own home. And I'm more than happy to tell you how I did it.

My technique involves a small room fitted with ordinary incandescent lights and a computer. On those balmy, blue-sky days when everyone else was outside walking, playing tennis, or lying on the beach in the sun, mindlessly developing tans that will plague them well into October, I'd go into that room. Then I'd close the door, turn on all the lights, fire up the computer, and write, sometimes for hours on end. Oh, sure, it takes discipline, and you have to be willing to give up some free time, but I figure that's the price you pay to look this good.

Even if you don't work at home like I do, you can still get pale. In fact, there's some evidence that the fluorescent lights normally found in commercial buildings may be even more effective than incandescent lighting. And there's no doubt that basking in the glow of a computer monitor will pale you faster than almost any other method. Just look at any programmer.

Some people find it convenient to work on their pallor during their lunch hours, eating tuna fish sandwiches at their desks while they finish overdue personnel reports. (If you've forgotten to pack a lunch, get something out of the vending machine. Eating food that comes wrapped in cellophane appears to help you pale faster. Again, just look at any programmer.)

Others find it easier to pale after five by extending their time in the office an hour or two, paling while they complete the sales figures for the next day's meeting. If you find you're just too pressed for time to pale during the week, consider working Saturdays and Sundays. Go in early and stay late.

Over your lunch hour, after work, or even on weekends, it doesn't matter when you get pale. However you choose to do it, a regular schedule of short sessions is always advisable. No one should try to get a pallor all in one afternoon. You have to do it gradually.

No, I didn't get this pale overnight, but it was worth every minute I spent on it. Now, when people enviously inquire, "Have you been on vacation? Where did you get that great pallor? You look terrific!" I don't say a thing. I just smile.

Underwear (Yes, Underwear!)

THE fashion word is out. And the word, in a word, is lingerie. I read that in a fashion mag. "With wonderful color," it said, "a decorative edge, and a sense of 'body' " (their punctuation, not mine).

Lingerie, of course, is nothing more than a six-dollar word for underwear. Which has always been called underwear because it's supposed to be what we wear under whatever we wear over the underwear. That's why they call it underwear. Because no matter what you wear over the underwear, the underwear is under there.

Well, not anymore it isn't. It isn't just the word that's out. The underwear is out, right out there where everybody can see it. (I know what you're saying. I can hear you. "Age," you're saying. "Age. It's just your age showing." No, it's not. What's showing isn't my age. It's underwear!)

It seems to me that all this underwear wearing started with Madonna. Surely you remember Madonna . . .

When Madonna was just beginning her career, she wore her underwear everywhere she went. A struggling artist, she was probably too poor to buy clothes to wear over her underwear. Anyway, it seemed to work so well for her that even after she started making money she kept on wearing her underwear everywhere, even though she could have bought overwear to wear over her underwear if she really had wanted to.

Next, clothing manufacturers started making overwear that looked like underwear, which resulted in twelve-year-old Madonna-wannabes going around looking like they were wearing their underwear when really they were just wearing clothes that looked like underwear, usually, because they still lived at home, over underwear that really was underwear. Some of them still do.

Now besides overwear that looks like underwear, we also have underwear that really *is* underwear. It just isn't completely under the overwear.

For example, in warm weather the boys around here wear shorts: regular, ordinary, nice-looking shorts. But under their shorts, they wear underwear shorts that are longer than their overwear shorts so that the underwear shorts hang out the bottom of the overwear shorts.

Professional basketball players do this. Grown men, seven-foot tall men with seven-figure salaries, wear underwear that hangs out from underneath their outerwear where God and everybody, including their mothers, can see it on national television. Their overwear shorts are shorter than their underwear shorts. And you know that with what they're making they could afford to spring for a couple more inches of material.

The girls around here wear shorts too, which makes sense especially in warm weather, except they sometimes wear their shorts over ankle-length, waffle-weave, thermal underwear, which makes no sense. And some of the shorts they wear over the underwear are men's boxer shorts, shorts that should be underneath something instead of outside over other underwear.

For a while some of the girls were wearing skirts with slips that were six inches longer than their skirts. (Now the skirts are six inches long, but that will change, probably by the time you read this.) There also were skirts that looked like slips but were really skirts and were worn over slips that looked like skirts but were really slips. (Got that?)

Now everybody, whether they're wearing shorts or skirts, wears undershirts everywhere: undershirts over outer shirts, undershirts over other undershirts, and undershirts under overshirts which are designed so that the undershirts show under the overshirts that look like undershirts.

Some high-fashion underwear is specifically designed to be worn under overwear that is so sheer you can see the underwear right through it or so short you can see . . . well, you get the idea.

Besides blush satin teddies, black garter panties, and waist-cincher petticoats, there are sheer and stretch-lace body suits, to be worn with nothing but skimpy skirts that look sort of like belts with ruffles. And then there's something called a slip dress, which looks just like you think it does only it's tighter and shorter than any reasonably well-fitting slip would be. It's sort of underwear that's worn as outer-wear and, as near as I can tell, usually without any underwear under there.

One season Calvin Klein showed a particularly fetching little (very little) number in silver lace for $730. "Lace," I read that year, "is the season's outstanding fabric." In this teeny tiny case, it was about $30 a square inch, which is pretty outstanding, just like the underwear, out standing where everybody can see it.

Given the cost, you should wear this outstanding dress out to no place less than the Met, or possibly Carnegie Hall, if somebody really important is playing something really good, like maybe Mozart. And you'll fit right in, even if you don't quite fit into the outer-underwear, because underwear that isn't under any other wear is everywhere any more. I just can't get used to it.

Shuffling to the Beat
of a Different Drummer

SHUFFLE-step, shuffle-step, ball change, ball change, brush back, hop, flap, shuffle-step. Reverse. "Get your weight forward," exhorts Lynda over the clatter of twenty-eight metal-clad feet.

Shuffle-step, shuffle-step, ball change, ball change, brush back, hop, flap, shuffle-step. We mutter it as we dance. "Up on your toes," she yells. "On your toes." Shuffle-step, shuffle-step, etc. "Don't stop! Keep moving," she shouts over the din.

We look at Lynda blithely tapping away in front of us. We look down at our feet, vainly commanding them to go faster. We look in the studio mirrors and quickly avert our eyes. We look silly.

We do this every Thursday. Time steps, cramp rolls. Pull-backs and draw-backs, double draw-backs and toe drops. Scuff, brush, shuffle, scuffle and riffle—a world of onomatopoeia. And steps with personalities and proper names. The Maxie Ford, the Susie Q, the Shuffle Off to Buffalo, and the Bombershay, known among us as (what else?) the Bumbershoot.

I can't quite remember exactly how it all started. Seems to me we were sitting around drinking one night when the subject of tap dancing somehow drifted lightly through the conversation. "You know," said Gene, just a tad sheepishly, "I've always wanted to learn how to tap dance."

"Me, too," said Andrea. "It looks like so much fun."

"Me, three," I added. "I've been wanting to take tap for years."

"I took tap," said Anne, "and it is fun. I loved it."

Somehow it was settled. We'd all take tap dancing together. We signed on, and there we were: four decidedly adult, and mostly middle-aged, persons—an accountant, a physical therapist, a German teacher, and *moi* in the back row of Tap I.

Of course, it does look like fun. And it is. It also looks possible, even easy. So smooth. Just one foot and then the other. Fred Astaire never sweats. Bill Robinson never frowns. Tap is a snap— you learn that from watching old movies. If a munchkin toting a full load of sausage curls and dimples can do it, so can we. Like Mike sings in *A Chorus Line*, "Make my feet go pitter-pat. Said 'I can do that, I can do that.' "

Well, sometimes we can do that . . . and sometimes we can't. A lot of the time we can't. We are amazingly inept, handily disproving the popular idea that people enjoy most what they do well. Though we started four years ago, we're still in Tap II, permanently plateaued. (We don't really expect ever to progress to Tap III—that's the professional track, full of community-theater stars and would-be Broadway hoofers. We have other goals.)

"Last week we did the Maxie Ford turn," says Lynda. "This week we're going to do cramp roll turns alternating with toe-heels." We groan. It doesn't matter. Toe-heels, Maxie Fords, cramp rolls, or even simple waltz clogs—done turning, they're impossible.

"As we age, our middle ears dry up," says Lynda, offering this information gratuitously as we struggle across the floor, single file. "That's why we have trouble turning when we get older." She doesn't mention names. She doesn't have to. We know who she's talking about.

Andrea, the youngest in our quartet, spins like a top. We try not to hold it against her. Gene and Anne and I all turn like some sort of long-neglected kitchen utensil, laboriously cranking around, unevenly and *very slowly*.

When we're not turning, however, our best speed is in the range of medium. Too slow and it's hard to keep your balance. We're best at time steps, but there are governors on our feet. They'll accelerate to a certain speed and that's it—the toes top out. Practice forever if you like, but the neurons won't fire any faster.

Tuesdays we practice in Gene's basement, pooling our collective memories, trying to piece together the routines Lynda gives us in class. We've learned dances to "Hello, Dolly," "The Varsity Drag," "Applause," and even Phil Collins's "Sussudio" (we didn't do well with that one—it went faster than our neurons). This session our dance is to Irving Berlin's "Let Yourself Go." Some would say we already have.

Does that start left or right? What comes after the second step-step-step ball change? Which beat is the brush on? This is the true meaning of thinking on your feet. We work hard for at least 45 minutes and then we go upstairs and sit at the kitchen table and drink wine.

At the office, Andrea taps by the copy machine. Gene taps up and down the aisles in his German classes. Anne does riffs in the hallway at work, and when I find myself alone in an elevator, I do time steps until I reach my floor.

The grand plan is that we'll tap full-time after we all retire. We'll combine our vocation with travel and become the first American geriatric tap troupe to tour Western Europe. Maybe we'll get a grant.

Gene will make travel arrangements and help us translate menus in restaurants. Anne will keep us all in shape, treating our injuries properly and giving massages when necessary. Since I lack any significant skills, I suppose I'll handle public relations.

As for Andrea, besides keeping the books, she's going to have to do all the turns. Sort of like backup singers in a classic Motown group, Gene and Anne and I, with our desiccated middle ears, will array ourselves behind her. And do time steps. At medium speed.

A Course, of Course

Don't bother calling. You'll only get the machine. No one's at home—not your mother, your father, your brother, your best friend Terry, or your next-door neighbor Melwin. Just like me, everybody's taking a class.

There are continuing education courses at your local high school, adult education offerings at the community college, wellness classes at your neighborhood hospital, and lifelong learning opportunities at libraries and churches. And no matter what your bent, one of them has just the course for you.

You can expand your aesthetic horizons with arts and crafts such as Intermediate Pumpkin Carving (fall semester only) and Creative Graffiti: Finding Your Personal Voice. Or sign up for the Special Pre-Holiday Workshop and make clever low-cost Christmas gifts from recycled toxic waste materials.

The culinary arts are extremely popular, with instruction available in everything from Microwave Tofu and Stir-Fried Jell-O Treats to Cuisines of Antarctica and Zimbabwean Provincial Cookery.

If you're interested in physical fitness, you can shape up and slim down with Dancercize, Prancercize, Walkercize, Talkercize (chat your way to a new you), Slimnastics, Swimnastics, or the latest exercise regimen for overweight middle-aged ethnics, Low-Impact Polkaerobics.

Intellectual stimulation and expanded career horizons can be yours with classes to teach you such valuable skills as Animal

Midwifery, Digital Numerology, and Disposable Ballpoint Pen Repair. Or sign up for one of these rewarding courses:

Sign Language Bird Calls: A one-evening seminar designed to help you communicate with our hearing-impaired feathered friends.

Easy-Does-It Jousting: Medieval war games for those over 60. Bring light-weight chain mail to first class. Note: Physician's permission is advised.

Pet Relaxation: Discover techniques to help your pet deal with the stresses of modern living. Course includes feline self-hypnosis and canine automassage.

Miniature Reactors: Build your own working model of a nuclear generating station. List of required tools and materials to be purchased will be mailed upon registration. Bring insurance waivers and disposable protective clothing to first class.

Creative Writing 1040: For long-form income tax filers. Concentrates on whimsical deductions and the structuring of interesting personae for fictional dependents.

Oral History: Preparing to meet with the auditors. Learn to support your filing position with colorful anecdotes and casual references to uninsured losses sustained while operating a tax-sheltered gerbil ranch in your garage. Prerequisite: Creative Writing 1040.

Transcendental Tap Dancing: Shuffle off to Nirvana. Course includes New Age rhythms for healing and time-stepping as an aid to meditation. Leg warmers and aromatherapy supplies may be purchased from instructor.

Community Kazoo Ensemble: Camaraderie and good music making for everyone. Ensemble rehearses weekly and performs concerts for nursing home residents and other captive audiences. No audition or musical skills required.

Beginning Organ Transplants: An absorbing hobby, or start a part-time career in this lucrative growth field. Class members must supply their own patients. Note: This is a ten-week course.

Conjugating for Peace

I AM not a scholar. In my day I was a facile, even glib, student, but I have never been a true scholar. I am not the kind of cerebral heavyweight who chooses thorny philosophical tomes as postprandial reading matter or tackles quadratic equations for their amusement value. And I have never even been tempted to memorize, as a musician friend of mine did, Homer's *Odyssey* in the original Greek.

So, consistent with a lifetime of intellectual shallowness, I did not begin studying Russian for the mental calisthenics. I began to learn at a fairly advanced age what can only be described as a very foreign language simply because I was going to be traveling in the land where it is spoken.

I started with a phrase book written for tourists, the sort of book that tells you how to ask for a clean fork or order theater tickets but doesn't clutter up your mind with irrelevant nonsense by explaining case endings and verb conjugations. I learned to say things like "What time does the concert start?" "I would like to buy two postcards" and "*Gday tooahlyet?*", i.e., "Where's the john?" (I also learned that "*M*" on the door means the same thing there as it does here and that I needed to be on the lookout for the door with the letter—not reproducible in this typeface—that looks sort of like a rococo X with Byzantine embellishments.) I learned to count to 20, noted the fact that five kopecks will take you anywhere on the Moscow Metro, and struggled with the Cyrillic alphabet only because I figured I might want to read a few street signs.

My plan was to learn absolutely no more than I needed to get by, but that's not the way it worked out. What did me in was that alphabet, 33 fascinating and frustrating characters that when I began made no more sense to me than a television evangelist's theology. A few, like M, K, and T, were familiar friends transplanted from the Roman alphabet. Many more letters were altogether new and strange, and, while I took some aesthetic pleasure in their fanciful forms, it seemed impossible to match them with the sounds they represent. Most troublesome were those politicians of the alphabet world, the letters that in their duplicity appear to mean one thing but say another. An H is really an N, a B sounds like a V, P is R, C is S, and an X is an H of sorts. We won't even talk about the backwards R or the Y that goes "ooo" like a Motown backup singer.

I began to suspect that the letters were part of an insidious Communist plot and that the right-wingers were correct. Not only was the empire evil, but the alphabet was too, its mission being to drive this one American raving crazy. I studied and I practiced, laboriously sounding out assigned lists of words—by then I was under the tutelage of a Russian-speaking friend—and getting nowhere.

Then one day, suddenly it all made sense. It was as if a Tom Mix genuine-tiger's-eye decoder ring (two cereal box tops and a quarter) had come in the mail. It felt like the mental equivalent of Rocky's victory over Apollo Creed. I had the power to unravel secret messages! I was special, I was *privy.* (I was hooked.)

Like a supermom friend of mine who was trying to teach her infant daughter French, I slapped labels on everything in the house. My sock and underwear drawers proclaimed *nahskee* and *troosih,* and *frooktih* and *ohvashchee* in the bottom of my refrigerator indicated whether the apples were hiding inside drawer number one or drawer number two. A sign on my bathroom mirror asked each morning "*Kahg dehlah?*" (Russian for "How's tricks?"), and I responded from a list of six possibilities ranging from "*ahtleech-nah!*" to "*oozhahsnah,*" which translates roughly as "My life's in the *tooahlyet.*"

I babbled incessantly, saying *"malakoh"* as I took the milk out of the *hadhlahdeelneek* and *"deevahn"* each time I sat down on the couch to watch the *televeesor*, driving my housemates completely nutzoid. I carried on inane conversations with myself ("What time is it? It is 11:20. Do you have a red book? Yes, I have a red book. My red book is on the table next to the lamp."), aware that I was butchering the case endings and scrambling the syntax, but forging ahead nevertheless.

A fascination for the sound of certain words overtook me— like *nahcheenahts* (to begin); *pochta* (post office); *chahshkah*, which sounds like an interesting name for a cat but means cup; and my favorite, *plahshch*, which approximates the sound of a close encounter with a puddle and means raincoat.

Russian words began to hop into my head unbidden. As I listened to a speaker talk about communication *between* individuals and *between* ethnic groups, *myehzdoo* flipped up at the front of my mind like the route sign on a bus. Playing Pictionary—a charade-like game in which you use drawings instead of physical movements for clues—I stopped the game cold by yelling out *"Ochkee!"* when my partner sketched a pair of glasses. (As I recall, the phrase he was trying to convey was "public spectacle.")

No longer concerned with what might be useful on the trip, I threw myself into the language indiscriminately. In church, sermons took on new meaning as I used the time to practice counting or name all the colors I could see. One Sunday I spent the sermon scrutinizing and enumerating, from my perch in the choir loft, the garments of the congregants below. (*Peedzhahk, roobahshka, bryookee, plahtyeh, bloozkah, yoobkah, sveetyar* . . . but not a *schlahpah* in the place. Hardly anybody wears hats anymore, at least not in a Unitarian church.) After a while I got bored and started to use my imagination to catalogue unseen slips, hankies, belts, stockings, and *troosih*. It was a new kind of spiritual enlightenment.

Stuffing my pockets with homemade flashcards, I studied Russian everywhere: waiting at the doctor's, on the subway, and in airports. I began to realize I enjoyed it in much the same way I enjoyed studying ballet, something I have spent much more time on than would appear seemly, given my obvious lack of talent. I liked it because it was so hard.

Of course, ten weeks does not fluency make. When the time came I went to the Soviet Union with a limited, if eccentric, vocabulary, speaking exclusively in the present tense and still butchering case endings. (The best strategy may just be to pretend you're from Alabama and slur the ends of all your words.)

I did purchase several postcards and, yes, I found the toilet. As it happens, I never needed to ask for a clean fork and I didn't order any theater tickets, but I was able to buy a ticket for a boat ride on the Neva River in St. Petersburg. I stepped off the beaten tourist track whenever possible and got myself into any number of lively half-mime, half-Russian conversations, including a fairly complicated one with a chambermaid in Minsk about why my laundry was returned unwashed.

My efforts were richly rewarded. I came home not only with a full load of dirty clothes but with the warm feeling that I probably had brightened the lives of myriad Soviet citizens. Given the entertainment potential of my fumbling attempts at Russian, I no doubt provided more moments of memorable comedy than I will ever know. In fact, I like to think of speaking Russian as my small contribution to world peace: international good will through inadvertent humor.

Epilogue:
Sympathy Pains

I T'S not easy being a humorist. Oh, sure, you can kid around all the time. You hardly ever have to dress up, a real plus in my book, and no one expects you to do any real work. (How hard can it be to write this stuff anyway, right?) You get to laugh a lot, be on the radio, and even have your name in the newspaper sometimes. Well, it has its down side, believe me.

I can cope with the adulation and high pay. That's not the problem. What gets me is that no matter what happens to me, I get no sympathy. Absolutely none. The worst fate in the world could befall me and I guarantee you, somebody would say, "This is going to make a really funny piece, isn't it?"

I can't complain about anything anymore without someone suggesting it would make a good column or a radio piece. Financial ruin, personal rejection, dire illness, lunch at Burger King, whatever. Instead of commiseration I get, "Never mind. You'll just write something funny about it." I could get run over by the 55X bus in the middle of Clifton Boulevard during rush hour on my birthday, and the first person who visited me in the hospital would say, "Boy, I can't wait to see what you write about this. I'll bet it'll be a real killer."

One of my best friends—also a writer, so she really ought to know better—always answers my tales of woe with, "Oh well, just more grist for the mill, dear." One of these days I'm going to strangle her. With my luck I'll be quickly tried and sentenced to die. The night before my execution the padre will come to see me on death row, but instead of assisting me with the passage of my immortal soul, he'll start telling me what terrific material I can get out of the experience. I'll probably strangle him, too. What would I have to lose?

It's true I've been able to glean a few laughs from the ghastly. I've written humorous pieces about such horrors as urban decay, viral pneumonia, February in Cleveland, and tofu. I even wrote a column about Ralph Nader once. I'm not above mining the appalling circumstances of my life for chuckles, but that doesn't mean I wouldn't like a little sympathy for them sometimes.

I was saying just this to a friend at lunch the other day. "Great," he said. "Oh, that's really funny. Death row. Ralph Nader. Tofu. I love it. Why don't you write a piece about it?"

I hope he doesn't read this.

Incomplete Index of Proper Names, Literary References, Scientific Terms, and Other Stuff

Incomplete Index

Indiana, a whole bunch of
different places
IRS, 11, 50, 149
Italians, 90

King, Burger, 154

Laundry, coin operated, 19, 62
Linkletter, Art, 112

MacNeil/Lehrer, 109
Mad Magazine, 132
Madonna, 142
Manners, Miss, 33, 110
Mauve, 20
Mental health, 11, 27, 94
Middens (not mittens), 88
Mittens (not middens), 82
Monaco, 1
Monster trucks, ESPN, weekdays
at 5
Mozart, 144
Mix, Bloody Mary, in the
refrigerator, top shelf
Mix, cake, above the stove
Mix, Tom, 152
"Muppet Babies," 106
Murray, Arthur, 64
"Muscle Magazine." *See* ESPN

NASA, 84
Nazca Plains, 81
Nemadi, 88

Ohio Department of Motor
Vehicles, 7
One-a-Day, 77
Organ transplants, 149

pH, 25
Phantom bomber, 17

Photosynthesis, 74
Platinum, price per pound. *See*
Turkey, smoked
Pizza, 109, 116
Pizza bagels, 13
Pizza, cold, 54
Pizza delivery, 64, or look in the
phone book

Quasimodo, 21
Queen Elizabeth. *See* Elizabeth,
Queen

Reagan, Nancy, 3, 29
Rivers, Joan. Not in MY book!
Robinson, Bill, 146
Rock Candy Mountain, Big, 81
Rocky, 152
Rocky and Bullwinkle, 132
Rotary Club, 95, 125
Rubber chickens, 68

Scholl's, Dr., 69
Schwarzenegger, Arnold, 120
Sears, 2, 68, 113, 120
Segal, Erich, 2
Smithsonian, 103, 114
Snellen chart, 64
Stoic. *See* Zeno
Sweat pants, 111

Tanglewood, 16
Tofu, 51, 59, 148, 155
Tories, 117
Tractor pulls. Get a life!
Trilobite, 24
Trombone, 95, 123
Turkey, smoked. *See* Platinum,
price per pound

Incomplete Index

You May Already Be a Winner
was composed on a Varityper system
in 10/13 Century Book with titles in Century Expanded
by Professional Book Compositors, Inc.;
printed by sheet-fed offset on 60-pound Glatfelter Natural
acid-free stock and adhesive bound
with paper covers printed in two colors and film laminated by
Edwards Brothers, Inc.;
designed by Will Underwood;
and published by
The Kent State University Press
Kent, Ohio 44242